An Introduction
to Child Drama

An Introduction to Child Drama

PETER SLADE

UNIVERSITY OF LONDON PRESS LTD

ISBN 340 0 11881 4

Seventh impression 1970

University of London Press Ltd
St Paul's House, Warwick Lane, London EC4

Printed and bound in England by
Hazell Watson and Viney Ltd, Aylesbury, Bucks

FOREWORD

In his major work, *Child Drama*, Mr. Slade has given us a very full analytical study of the creative drama in which children, if unhampered by imposition from adults, can find expression of themselves and so reach towards the full development of their personality. This valuable book has been widely read and discussed by teachers both in this country and overseas.

In this new book, *An Introduction to Child Drama*, all the fundamental principles of Mr. Slade's methods are clearly and simply stated with abundant practical illustration. It is an excellent exposition of the subject and should undoubtedly whet the appetite of the reader to explore it further in the larger book.

For many experienced teachers, with a knowledge of children and of drama, much of the ground covered will be familiar, but even they will find reassurance, refreshment and stimulus in these pages. For the young teacher, and for those who lack confidence in their own imaginative perceptiveness, this book should be invaluable.

Mr. Slade writes from a wide experience and patient observation of children. His approach to them is analytical, but his attitude throughout the book is infused with a warm humanity and sympathy and the words "love" and "enjoyment" occur frequently. I find what the author has to say about the relationship between child drama and child art particularly interesting; and his advice to parents should prove of special value.

I have had the opportunity of seeing a little of the work done in Infant, Junior and Secondary Modern schools, by teachers who have studied under Mr. Slade, and there is no doubt that the method "works". I saw some remarkable spontaneous dance. One small boy of ten years danced— with a group, yet "on his own"—with a grace and a joyful exaltation which was unforgettable. In a boys' Secondary School I was impressed by the effortless control which the children themselves seemed to exercise with no apparent help from the teacher. A wildly exciting game of smugglers pursued by police in motor-launches raged all over the hall and stage, but there were no casualties, and quite suddenly it all ended and melted into quietness. There was no need for the teacher to blow a whistle or shout to them to stop.

To me, one of the most valuable things in this book is where the author makes this statement (p. 74):

"It may be found that some form of social drama in this sense is the best way to start things off with older children who have already become self-conscious. They have a spurious contempt for art as such, but if neither the words *drama* nor *theatre* were stressed they might be very prepared to discuss and practise preparation for life, and particularly life after school. It makes them feel grown-up. Once having become released, they can be more easily introduced to other parts of drama as a whole."

I have found in many schools that there is a failure to carry on the "creative" approach into the scripted play. The same teacher may encourage creative class-room drama and then apply a completely different technique in rehearsals of the "school play", whereas the method should be recognisably the same in both. The actor, whether child, adolescent or adult, should from the first look upon drama as being, doing and living characters in plays as real people in real life. But too often the printed word gets in the way, and the play is approached as something to be read, then learnt by heart, and then recited aloud, while the teacher or producer "puts in the expression" and "adds gestures", all of which the actor never relates to human experience. Mr. Slade, in insisting that the approach to the scripted play should come through improvised "social drama", provides quite clearly the "link" between improvisation and formal drama which some educationists appear to find difficult. There should be no "gap" here to be bridged. The whole process of imaginative development into drama as a form of art should be continuous, for the child and the artist are akin, and the adult artist retains throughout his work the single-minded absorption of the child.

It is to be hoped that an increasing number of teachers in all types of schools will work along the lines suggested by Mr. Slade in this admirable book. When that happens it should be possible to observe the results of continuity in development of the creative artist from childhood into adult life.

FRANCES MACKENZIE
former Principal,
British Drama League
Training Department

PREFACE

MANY PEOPLE, at home and abroad, have asked me for a short version of *Child Drama*. This book is an attempt to answer their need. Most of the work is new, though some passages are from the first book, more particularly where the original words seemed the best to illustrate a point. There are some fresh examples from schools, and many of the photographs have not been published before. A special section is written for parents, because of the growing interest shown by Parent-Teacher Associations.

I am grateful to Mr. Brian Way for help in selecting and arranging material; to Mr. Victor Thompson for taking photographs, sometimes under difficult conditions; and my thanks are also due to Birmingham Education Committee for allowing use of pictures and descriptions of work in some of their schools.

A shortened version is always apt to leave out the very points a reader would wish to find and I am very conscious of probable failings in this respect. Nevertheless I hope that this short book may prove of value as an introduction to the subject, which is not only about theatre as we understand it but mostly about the kind of drama that children themselves create, and how it can be guided into constructive channels by the sympathetic adult.

PETER SLADE

CONTENTS

PLATES

ACKNOWLEDGMENT

The author and publishers make grateful acknowledgment to Victor Thompson and Cater's News Agency Ltd., Birmingham, for permission to use the photographs reproduced in this book.

CHAPTER I

GENERAL PRINCIPLES

CHILD DRAMA is an art form in its own right; it is not an activity that has been *invented* by someone, but the actual behaviour of human beings.

This book is a short introduction to the subject, a more comprehensive survey of which is contained in *Child Drama*.[1] Here I have attempted to outline a method of planned emotional training, based upon some thirty years' observation of children at play. When considering the art form of Child Drama it is necessary for us, as adults, to differentiate between what the child in actual fact does and what we know and understand as theatre; and because the root of Child Drama is *play*, it is with play that we must largely concern ourselves in the first instance.

Play, not Theatre

Play is an inborn and vital part of young life. It is not an activity of idleness, but is rather the child's way of thinking, proving, relaxing, working, remembering, daring, testing, creating and absorbing. It is, in fact, life. The best child play takes place only where opportunity and encouragement are consciously given to it by an adult mind. This is a process of nurturing and is not the same as interfering. It is necessary to build confidence by friendship, and the right atmosphere by sympathetic consideration.

[1] *Child Drama* by Peter Slade; published by University of London Press Ltd.

In this child play, there are moments of such clear characterisation and emotional situation that a further term has arisen: dramatic play. This always seems a good term to use, for in thinking of children, particularly young ones, a distinction should be made most carefully between *drama* in the wide sense and *theatre* as understood by adults. Theatre means an ordered occasion of entertainment and shared emotional experience; there are actors and audience—differentiated. But the child, if unspoiled, feels no such differentiation, particularly in the early years—each person is both actor *and* audience. This is the importance of the word *drama* in its original sense, coming from the Greek word *drao*—"I *do*, I *struggle*." In drama—i.e. *doing* and *struggling*—the child discovers life and self through emotional and physical attempt, and then through repetitive practice, which is dramatic play. The experiences are exciting and personal, and can develop into group experiences. But in neither the personal nor the group experience is there any consideration of theatre in the adult sense, unless *we impose it*. There may be intense moments of what we would deign to call theatre, but in the main it is drama, and the adventure, doing, questing and struggling are tried by all. *All* are *doers*, both actor and audience, going where they wish and facing any direction they like during play. Action takes place all about us, and there is no question of "who should act to whom and who should sit and face whom doing what"! It is a virile and exciting experience, in which the teacher's task is that of a loving ally. And in this drama, two important qualities are noticeable—*absorption* and *sincerity*. Absorption is being completely wrapped up in what is being done, or what one is doing, to the exclusion of all other thoughts, including the awareness of or desire for an audience. Sincerity is a complete form of honesty in portraying a part, bringing with it an intense feeling of reality and experience, and only fully achieved in the process of acting with absorption.

We should foster these qualities by all the means in our power because they are of extreme importance to the growing individual (and also, incidentally, because they will improve all attempts at theatre if they are kept alive after puberty). The qualities begin to emerge in even the early stages of the two main forms of play—*personal* play and *projected* play.

Personal and Projected Play

Some child observers would make a distinction between *realistic* play and *imaginative* play. But, in fact, play (certainly in the earlier stages) is so fluid, containing at any moment experiences of everyday outward life and of inner imaginative life, that it is debatable whether the one should be distinguished as a different activity from the other. It is important, of course, that the difference is understood, but the distinction pertains more to the intellect than to play itself. The healthy child develops towards reality as it gains experience of life. This is a process rather than a distinction. *The only true distinction in play is that of* personal *play and* projected *play*.

PROJECTED PLAY	PERSONAL PLAY
Projected play is drama in which the whole mind is used, but the body is not used so fully. Treasures[1] are used which either take on characters of the mind or become part of the place ("stage" in a theatre sense) where drama	*Personal play* is obvious drama; the whole person or self is used. It is typified by movement and characterisation, and we note the dance entering and the experience of being things or people.

[1] By *treasures* are meant dolls, bricks, old paper, etc.—in fact, any object upon which love is momentarily poured or upon which affection (somewhat difficult to understand) is lavished for long periods.

PROJECTED PLAY—*cont.*

PERSONAL PLAY—*cont.*

happens. In typical projected play we do not see the whole body being used. The child stands still, sits, lies prone or squats, and uses chiefly the hands. The main action takes place outside the body, and the whole is characterised by extreme mental absorption. Strong mental projection is taking place.

In personal play, the child journeys about and takes upon himself the responsibility of playing a rôle.

In projected play the tendency is towards quietness and physical stillness. The objects played with, rather than the person playing, take on life and do the acting, though there may be vigorous use of voice.

In personal play the tendency is towards noise and physical exertion on the part of the person involved; and if noise is not employed, exertion is.

Projected play is mainly responsible for the growing quality of absorption.

Personal play develops the quality of sincerity, by absolute faith in the part portrayed.

Projected play is more evident in the early stages of a young child, who is not yet ready to use his body fully.

Personal play should be quite apparent by five years of age, and becomes more frequent and easier to distinguish as mastery of the body is achieved.

The child who has the right opportunities will try out in personal and projected play many fragments of thought and experience between the ages of one and five years, and although absorption will be far ahead of sincerity, the two qualities combined will be strong enough for even the somewhat unobservant to perceive moments of unmistakable acting.

Thus drama—always there, always vital, always beautiful—proceeds slowly from the less obvious to the more obvious and thence to the unmistakable, though certain characteristics are recognisable throughout.

These two main forms of play add qualities to each other, and also to the person who plays. Throughout the whole of life Man is happy or unhappy in so far as he discovers for himself the right admixture of these quite distinct manners of using energy. Both the type of person and the life occupation are connected with the balance of self and projection. These two early types of play have an important bearing on the building of Man, his whole behaviour, and his ability to fit in with society. Play opportunity, therefore, means gain and development. Lack of play may mean a permanent lost part of oneself. It is this unknown, uncreated part of oneself, this missing link, which may be a cause of difficulty and uncertainty in later years. (For this and other reasons, backward children often respond to further opportunities for play, by which they build or rebuild self, doing at a later stage what should have been done before.)

Out of *projected* play, we may expect to develop later: art, playing musical instruments, love of fresh-water fishing, non-violent games (from snakes and ladders to chess), reading and writing.

Observation, patience, concentration, organisation and wise government.

To these should be added interest in puppets, model theatres, and, in the full sense, play production.

Speech and music are employed, sometimes intermittently, sometimes as a running commentary.

Out of *personal* play, we may expect to develop later: running, ball games, athletics, dance, riding, cycling, swimming, fighting, hiking, etc. These are all forms of acting.

Leadership and personal control are developed.

To these should be added acting in the full sense. Child acting contains these things, too, sometimes before the actor knows how to do them. Imagination and copying are mixed.

Speech and music are employed.

In both types of activity there are discernible shapes which are important for us to observe.

Recurring Shapes

The one predominant shape that can be seen very frequently is the *circle*. It appears even at the baby stage, when we can observe it in early crawling and later in running, in turning round on one spot, and in a certain stamping and jigging, particularly in puddles, which will one day turn into dance if we help it to grow.

Between five and seven years we see circles widening, and in infant schools there appears the really big co-operative circle with nearly everyone in it, and also the filled-in circle with everyone running round.

At about seven years or a little before, the gang stage becomes apparent because companions are an important part of normal life at this age. The gang develops round a leader with a strong self, not yet quite ready to integrate with the group. (The strong self is an intermediate personality between child and adult for the other members of the gang.) With the gang stage, the circle splits up into smaller circles. These are both symbolic of and symptomatic of the gang itself, and often comprise actual members of a close social relationship.

The circle in varying forms is still seen between eleven and thirteen years, but after that there comes naturally, if unhurried, a genuine inclination towards theatre as we know it. A raised stage may be useful at this time, but a wide floor space to aid free movement is still the chief necessity.[1] If creation is left unhampered when a stage is used, there will be a robust flowing on and off the stage

[1] Do not be discouraged if you have not a wide floor space; there is much that can be done without one, as will be explained in later chapters.

in a kind of tongue shape. There *must* be stairs or rostra at the front of the stage to ensure that this movement is free.

INFANTS	JUNIORS	SENIORS
Typical big circle of infants; some smaller ones beginning.	Small circles appear more frequently (seven years plus).	About thirteen plus; stage is used sometimes, but there is strong flow on or off. This is the tongue shape.

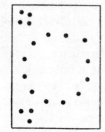 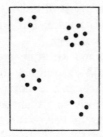 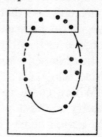

There are other discernible and regular shapes at certain ages:

In the infant school there is the *spiral*; this is always the shape of happy entry into the hall when, in response to sound,[1] the children run or dance joyfully in, forming a spiral shape. In this, as in much of their movement, they run to the left with their hearts towards the centre of the room, possibly because their right legs are stronger. We also see in the infant and junior schools a ragged circle running round, and the S shape, which is half of a figure 8 common in running play. Running play does not happen very often—never in a school where young children are made to work on a stage—but shows great artistry at the peak of its development with eight- or nine-year-olds. At sudden and special moments a child will break for sheer

[1] See Chapters II and III

joy into a run, whether acting or dancing. Knees bent, arms held out like wings, with great absorption and an ecstatic expression, the child moves swiftly and rhythmically in a snake-wise or figure-8 shape, and pays great attention to the sound of feet and to some moment of intended climax, which can be helped and encouraged if a rostrum block is lying about somewhere in the hall.

From twelve to thirteen plus years we see small gang groups in front of the stage, but still not using it; and at fourteen years there is a sort of bulge, which is practically the use of proscenium theatre, but with use of the fore-stage or of flowing down steps.

In cramped classrooms we often see the three-quarter circle, which is the child's attempt to make a full circle.

Where there is space and opportunity, we see great beauty in the flow of movement as each individual draws the actual chart of his or her own progress on the floor space. It is this "chart" and its relationship to other journeys of other individuals that we should watch with the greatest care during play, for it tells us in detail, as by graph, of personal and social attainment. It is best viewed and "read" from above.

Relation between Art (Projected Play) and Drama

An interesting and important fact is that painting and drawing improve in proportion to the sense of space discovered in movement over the floor. A young child who may be seen to run in an S-shape, or star, or triangle shape, is also producing these shapes on paper at this age, and, as bumping into companions in movement on the floorspace ceases, so pictorial composition improves. This is because children are beginning to sort out the difference between mass and space by experiencing it three-dimensionally (*personal* play). They notice their own body and the span between themselves and each other person. With the practice that drama brings, bumping ceases earlier, and this in turn brings about improvement of the art. Art therefore is, as it were, a thermometer chart of where the person has got to in development (*projected* play); the "chart" can be read by the experienced eye, even if the drama does not make it obvious.

When children have discovered and sorted out space, in the physical sense, and at the same time are wanting to be more serious about their drama in the emotional and aesthetic sense, they then achieve *equidistance*. This appears both in the use of floorspace (personal play) and in the art (projected play). It is a step in the direction of mental tidiness and growing-up, and it is also an important social advancement as children begin to consider the needs of others. And, of course, they can be helped to do this.

In art, equidistance is the forerunner of what is termed composition, where mass, colour and space are more purposefully and intellectually arranged. Composition is always better where the equidistance stage has been passed through properly, because the full three-dimensional experience of drama makes a need in the child's mind for good composition. The parallel of composition in art is good grouping in drama.

In all the child's simple drama activity we find qualities of form and evidence of a skill, though much of it is unconscious. For my own part, because of these and many other reasons (the whole philosophy of which is set out in the complete work,[1]) I have no hesitation in affirming that there exists in fact a *Child Drama* that is an art form in its own right, which should be recognised, respected, nurtured and developed.

[1] *Child Drama*, Part I.

CHAPTER II

WHAT PARENTS CAN DO TO HELP

CHILD DRAMA is a form of expression that concerns the whole nature of man. Children become happy, confident and obedient by using drama, and wise adults, by watching it, see how far a child has got in life. For it is life itself —the whole mental and physical growth of young beings —that this art form is really concerned with. By knowing about Child Drama our attitude to people may change and our understanding deepen. It is therefore of great importance to all parents as well as teachers, so we begin with a few remarks on the attitude of parents and the needs of a baby.

General Attitude of Parents

The most important thing in a baby's life is love. It sounds too obvious. But love can be elusive or of the wrong kind. A baby must be wanted before and after it is born. Things done for the child should be done for its real need and not for the sentimental whim of the parents. It is necessary to find a balance of affection so that the child is not overwhelmed by emotion one minute and actively disliked the next. Just like the teacher in a child's later life, the parent should not try to be a saint, but discover early how to form an even pattern of personality-behaviour towards children, a mixture of patience and affection.

Don't be afraid of psychology. Because you are advised to give affection and may fear to thwart, that does not mean that you need not obtain obedience. To allow misunderstanding over obedience in the early years is un-kind. It does not help the child. Make few rules, but see they are obeyed, kindly but firmly. Let them become custom.

Mother should do most of the guiding. Father should be the last big gun, the final authority. Don't let this position slip or you will destroy confidence in the family atmosphere.

Remember, language is an emotional thing for children. "Yes" and "No" are learnt not only for their meaning, but as emotional music. There is something profoundly uncertain-making if they mean and feel one thing one moment and another the next. That is the simple insecurity which is at the root of some troubles in later life. Don't be afraid. Yes means *Yes* and No means *No*. See that your children understand. Correction is better done by tone of voice than by smacking. But don't roar all day. Keep your trump cards for the needed moment.

Don't expect your children to be clean all the time. They must get dirty during some forms of play as they will in some forms of work when grown up. Washing comes after. For everything and everybody to be clean as a new pin all the time may mean self-satisfaction for the keen housewife, but it can be an unhealthy tyranny for children. Learn to decide about appropriate occasions for cleanliness.

Don't over protect your children by being too nervous to let them out of your sight. Notice that they are growing up. Don't continually do things for them. Say often: "See if you can do it." Encourage, but don't leave a child stranded and hopeless. There is a balance for each little person. They will all be different. But the balance is not too difficult to find, as a rule, once you are aware of its existence.

There should be a sense of community in a good home, a sense of fun, the feeling that everyone has a chance to try things out in his own way, and a sense of security.

In all our dealings with children we should continually say to ourselves: "If I were *really* that little person in that position, what would I do, what would I think, what would I say?" The greater your power of perception in this line of thought the more disinterested will be your love, and the more understanding you will become.

Children apply just this attitude to their play. They start with the same honesty of thought, only with them it is simpler, more straightforward, because they are young. They think: "If I were really that flying dragon, that spaceman or that atomic sausage, *I* would do this and say that." They do it, and that is Child Drama. Their manner of carrying out the thought is their art form. We should observe it and encourage it, for there is an unfolding pattern of human behaviour by which Man discovers himself and learns to think of others.

We have already seen that there are two main kinds of play: one where children play with objects and often make them live (*projected play*), the other when children themselves become the imagined people, animals or things (*personal play*).

Projected play is more common in the early years. Later, according to the amount of absorption that the parent has allowed, this play can be guided by sensible teachers into careful study at lesson time. It has by then been built into a habit of concentration. (Note: Grammar stream places depend as much on these early formative years as on the last uncomfortable cramming.) Some of the building of concentration by imaginative means continues in school, too.

Personal play is catered for less. Its beginnings are often

not noticed, or even discouraged, because it needs space and generally includes declamation. Both these forms of play may be drama, but not necessarily theatre as adults understand it. Drama is less obvious in projected than in personal play, though there are moments of clearly defined drama going on when sticks and stones or dolls live and have a voice. These objects are often left in a primitive pattern after play. The pattern is a sort of symbol of the living story that went on in the child's mind, whether speech came out or not. This is also what happens when pictures are painted.

Personal play develops as children attain more control of their body and mastery over the objects they play with. For children, their own type of drama means the whole of the doing of life, and this is their natural and best way of developing movement and speech. The quality which they develop in this type of play is *sincerity*. It is a deep quality of the character and starts in the earliest years. It is often at the very moment when complete confidence in actually living *fully* could be attained in this way that children are squashed because of an adult-ordered world. So many of us therefore, unknowingly, cause the precise problems in children that we later deprecate. For they will find other ways of expressing themselves, which may be less desirable, and often away from adult supervision. Sometimes the public form of expression is a built-up negative attitude to life, rather too common amongst young people at the moment.

Some Detailed Suggestions for Assisting Child Drama at Home

Allow: Banging noises sometimes (from babyhood upwards). Interest yourself in the many different types. Only take away what is dangerous, or will be spoiled, by drawing the child's attention to something else. Don't snatch.

Reason: Children love sound. They divide it into time-beat, rhythm and climax. They find out many things about speech, music and drama that you don't know about by testing sounds in their own way.

What the adult can do: Give delight by joining in sometimes. Use other noises. Don't irritate the child by taking his toy and showing how it "should" be played with. Lead slowly on to a distinction between loud and soft sounds, long sounds and percussive sounds.

Examples: Bits of metal on string; tapping bits of wood and cardboard; stretched elastic noise; rice in a tin.

Think in terms of question and answer. Answer the child's "statement" in sound. Just do it. Don't talk about it. Enjoy it and you will find that children not only follow you towards civilisation but lead you into a world you didn't know about. As children get older, let them see that there are times when you want to be quiet. There must be compromise and thought for others, particularly in small homes. You can train children, but don't destroy them. You don't need to be a musician for all this. Just be human and have serious fun.

Allow: Jumping up and down and standing sometimes (from babyhood upwards). Allow running about. Don't stop all running because you are afraid your child will fall down; it will, but it has got to learn how not to. Comfort it if disaster occurs, and help arrange soft falling places if you can, or stand by ready to catch. But don't always prevent. Don't force a baby to walk longer than it wants to or before it wants to. Encourage.

Reason: Jumping and stamping lead to an interest in athletics later and are the basis of Child Dance. They are the first steps towards personal style and discovery of personal bodily rhythm which helps to save energy throughout life and may affect ability in cricket, tennis, football, etc., in years to come. Forcing brings distaste and occasionally does some physical harm.

The adult can: Take an interest in the kinds of jumping and stamping. Occasionally join in, in time, occasionally to a different time. Don't infer that the child is wrong. Think sometimes in terms of question or statement and answer. Stamp back. The child will generally stamp again (this is the parallel in personal play to noise-making with objects). Use objects sometimes yourself, and mix the two kinds of play. Inspire the child to further movement by the sounds you make. This is the C—A—T of messages in sound. It is more important than the piano to start with. Longer sentences of sound should come later.

Allow: The occasional shouting and spitting and blah-blah talk of babies and very young children.

Reason: It is part of the discovery of lung power, feeling the palate and search for diction and "placing forward" of speech.

The adult can: Answer sometimes in blah-blah talk. You can carry on emotional conversations of supreme gaiety or of purple-faced seriousness even with babies this way, and a strong bond of understanding is built for short moments. Occasionally put in a real word. Repeat it. Later the child will use it and extend its tiny vocabulary. Base all speech and music and communication on a *deep love of sound*. This is what leads to a really intelligent taste in literature later. It is the true way to genuine appreciation of poetry. Too much jogging up and down and use of sentimental rhyming jingles leads to "versification", which is different, and to some understanding of time-beat. It does *not* lead to an appreciation of live rhythm and true poetic perception.

Allow: The making up of odd new words. Don't call them rubbish.

Reason: This creation starts because of interest in language. "Real" words are equally loved later.

The adult should: Accept new words. Learn to recognise the good ones. Some are very descriptive. Keep a few as family words and use them. They form a bond of "home" between the family.

Allow: Games about cowboys and gangsters and some dressing-up (as the children grow out of the toddler stage). Do not scorn it at home or make fun of it before visitors.

Reason: This is the real stuff. This is the drama by which an extension of vocabulary for expressing ideas is developed, by which emotions are thrown out, and in which a child tries all sorts of personalities until he discovers his own. He tries out *life* and finds himself. He creates a great art form of acting, too, both amusing and beautiful.

The adult should: Understand that your child is not a potential delinquent because a lot of killing happens during play. He or she is overcoming the imagined adversary. You want your child to win battles in life, don't you? This is practice and preparation for it. Long may they overcome! Take it seriously. If a child speaks to you as if you were subject to its kingship, you are being offered a confidence. Answer as a courtier should and keep the sincerity there; the better you behave, the better will you teach how one *should* behave in appropriate moments in life, which is being practised very deeply at these moments.

If you have a gramophone, put on music with pronounced time-beat or exciting passages in it, during the acting. The music will inspire. Don't be upset if children talk while it is on. They should talk in their drama. They only draw on the sound emotionally at first. Later you can lead them to some further selection, and may become companion enough to them to suggest a march-tune for part of a march round, etc. Better still, just put it on when they *are* marching, and be ready to take it off when they have finished. You will become more and more clever at this by practice and, as you get to know Child Drama better, you will learn to guess their needs in advance. It is useful to have these categories of music by you: gay, exciting, sad and calm.

Finish up with "gay" if the children seem moderately exhausted, or if you can still carry on giving them of your time and self after the game. Otherwise use "calm". This will often quieten them and they will be more likely to run off and play amongst themselves quietly. You will be aiding the teacher at school, too. For a sensible teacher will always finish a session of Child Drama with a calm feeling so as to prepare children for projected activity in the form of three-R work. You will be preparing children for this experience or helping to establish the good habit.

Allow: Other children to join yours in Child Drama if they want to and if you think you can manage them.

Reason: Children learn tolerance by playing together. By proper use of Child Drama you will teach them to be obedient, too, by arranging for their emotional activity to take place in a legitimate way under sympathetic supervision rather than by trying to dominate them. So many children are longing for this, without quite knowing it. All children need it. Many have homes or parents that make the whole business difficult. Sometimes the whole atmosphere of a street or village can be changed by one kindly, imaginative grown-up arranging times for drama of this kind.[1] If you become interested in this kind of play, a

[1] This subject is developed in detail in the section "Out of School" in *Child Drama*, Part III.

golden rule is: If there is a need, *the grown-up may suggest what to do; but don't show how to do it.*

Don't interrupt play. Talk about an episode afterwards if the children wish.

Some "Don'ts"

Don't give your children too many expensive toys. Give paints, paper, and simple things. Give them happiness.

Don't encourage showing off. Share success. Don't watch it too much.

Don't encourage ideas of theatre in early years. Everybody works in Child Drama. There is normally no audience. An audience brings self-consciousness.

Don't force a child to take part. Encourage.

Don't clear up things too regularly without thought. Notice if things are arranged in a pattern. A child may want to come back to it.

Don't ridicule any dramatic oddity or attempt at dance.

Don't thoughtlessly discuss your children with other adults. They have ears. They can be hurt.

Don't use puppets too much. The child himself needs to act.

Don't think your child must automatically be sent to a theatre school, ballet mistress or tap-dance expert, because it indulges in dramatic play. Grace can be achieved by practice in the child's own form of imaginative dance. The other things, as with all formal work, are not fundamentals but perfections. They do not suit everybody and may give some children the wrong idea.

Some "Do's"

Do leave strange things stuck in odd places if you can without too much untidiness. Father will know how he feels when his study or workroom is tidied, and everything put neatly where he can't find it. What would you feel if you were a "cowboy" and someone pinched the rope you had hung on the armchair or tree? The cows might escape. Then what? Make a mental note and see things are collected at the end of the day. Tidiness can be learned without sorrow.

Do provide a room for children to be apart from adults some of the time if you possibly can, where they can leave a few things "to be continued" next day.

Do allow young children a moment or two to finish what they are doing if they are deeply immersed in a task. You will learn to judge whether they are intentionally being disobedient or merely absorbed. The latter is no sin, it is a virtue. Later they can learn to snap out of it more easily.

Do let children take up their own grouping during play. It will be all about the room or garden and a circle will often be formed. Places of far distance may be quite close in this drama. Avoid saying things like "Don't turn your backs", as if you were dealing with proscenium theatre.

Do encourage children to improvise their speech and stories.

Do be ready for a quick change of character. Avoid laughing if a five-year-old becomes five different people or things in a matter of seconds. If you are asked to be a sign-post or a nail—*be* it.

Do refrain from laughing at the wrong moment (if by any chance you are asked to attend a school play). You destroy sincerity of portrayal and absorption in the acting and the atmosphere of the play. It is hard enough for any children under eleven years of age to attain these things in formal work, anyway. Don't make it harder.

Do try to learn a little about ray-guns and outer-space language. Don't be disapproving. You will cut yourself off from their confidence if you are (it may all become true in their lifetime, anyway), but will surprise and please them as an unexpected companion if you learn it. You may become the good gang leader, the leader all juniors unconsciously need. It is not always their fault that they come under the sway of a bad one. It may be the only one they meet. You cannot and should not quite take the place of a young leader, but you can show an example of good pattern.

Do encourage your children to be interested in life and beauty.

Encourage them to be clean and polite on appropriate occasions and at the same time to be courageous and virile. These attitudes arise largely from parental influence and home background. Avoid saying things like: "Oh, I shouldn't do that, dear." Are you one of those? Think hard. Get into the habit of considering what is the reason for the child *not* to do that. Was it just that you would be disturbed? One can learn to be positive: "All right, dear. Try." Such is the home which produces the confident adult. In a somewhat decadent world, modern life is crying out for a generation which will do and dare and take responsibility. Let your children say: "I'll try anything once." Your job is to help them to see what is sensible, to try it and to succeed.

Games

With babies: Peep Bo! But don't put your face too close to theirs suddenly. Don't remain hidden long.

Make funny people with your hands.

Toddlers and older children: Carry on a conversation in noises only.

Pull the ugliest face you can think of and act a story about it. (Or the nicest face.) Don't stay ugly long.

Tell a story round a circle of people, each one carrying on quickly from the next. Act it afterwards if desired.

Describe things in the room, a sort of "I Spy". But when you come to it pull a face or make a noise instead of saying the thing. We must guess what it is. Elaborations can take place, too. Example: "I spy with my little eye ..." or "Je perceive avec mon grand space lamp (a horrible face is here pulled) over a (slam noise)." It will turn out that the object is a clock or picture over the door.

Dolls' tea-parties or royal feasts.

Puppet tea-parties and/or Olympic Games (not in a theatre. All about the room).

Cut out simple paper-masks. Cut away nose, eyes and mouth. Put on masks. Dab paint on nose and mouth. Take off the masks. Act what the extraordinary resulting people with coloured faces remind you of. Of course, the masks might have started things off. But children generally discard the masks if they are full ones, because they are too hot and difficult to see through.

Beat a drum or a box and kill an enemy at each "bonk". Kill them hard. Overcome the *whole world* and all your troubles.

Get children to give you ideas in one or two words. Make up a short story to act from the ideas (see also description on page 35). Put on a record and (*a*) let people be what they think; (*b*) tell a story about what the music says; (*c*) just dance the story in your own way.

Hold a Red Indians' feast. Dressed-up war dances after tea to drum-beats and music.

Hold a gymkhana on the lawn, with pretend horses and real jumps (and sweets or dandelions for prizes, if you are doing the whole affair properly).

Hold a motor-race meeting to hot jazz and a megaphone. (Bicycles, scooters, soap-boxes, barrows, etc., for outside. Just yourselves for inside.)

Hold a pirates' regatta.

Hold a policeman's sausage party. (It can give certain children quite a different and improved idea of the Law.)

Hold a tea-party to meet the first "Martians". (Atomic pop will be laid on. Please bring your space guns.)

Act stories out of a newspaper, book or magazine.

For Sunday, consider acting stories out of the Bible.

As the drama improves you will be able to pop in an extra idea from them or yourself every now and again to enrich the whole creation. With a little dressing-up, some music added, and as long as you have fostered the qualities of sincerity and absorption, you will begin to perceive a grave innocence of demeanour and a grace of movement, a consideration for others and a sense of constructive co-operation. The whole adds up to a pageant of beauty that is difficult to describe. It is a glimpse of another world.

CHAPTER III

WHAT TO DO WITH INFANTS

ALL children are creative artists. Do not think that because they copy some things from life that it argues
against this; they bring in life experience for enrichment,
testing and proving. But think hard before offering them
powerful things, such as our theatre, to copy too early in
their lives.

Let us start at, say, five years of age, before which
every attempt has been made to avoid showing off, and
to *share* the child's experiences rather than look at them.
At five years continue to avoid theatre, stages and
scripts. The child is going to create with our help, so we
are going to stimulate improvisation—improvised movement, situation and language. I would do it by using
sound.

Children love sound, and, by using various interesting
noises in the infant school, we can inspire them to create
in their own manner. They divide sound in three main
ways—time-beat, rhythm and climax (we can build a
bond with them more easily if we understand this), so it
is in this way that I shall use the things I am taking into
the hall: drums, gongs, whistles, old tins, sandpaper, two
sticks, etc. I may sometimes use a piano or a gramophone,
but rather in the later stages.

*Example 1—I should start by making sounds in the hall
before the children enter.*

Reason: They enter then with curiosity and pleasure.
Because children hear sound emotionally they take joy in

it, and joy is necessary for their best creation. When they
become used to the work the entrance shape will be in a
spiral, all running with their hearts towards the centre.
The big circle follows, then the filled-in one as all move
round. (See diagram on page 7.)

I stop making the sound. All movement stops. I now
have full attention without any comments. I shake some
small bells.

Self: "What does this remind you of?"

A child: "Sleigh bells."

Self: "Yes, *look* at the snow. Your sleigh would pull nicely.
Are you ready? Pull!"

> Several children begin to pull, some perhaps to
> trot round. *All* are creating, not just the little show-
> offs picked out. I give no directions but just alter the
> speed of the bells, slowing down when I judge fit. The
> children obey the sound. They are learning about
> climax, and a little about mood, and a little about
> absorption, i.e. concentration for study as well as
> good acting. I blow a whistle.

Self: "What was that?"

Child: "A train."

Another: "Please, a hot kettle."

Self: "Quite right, a train with a kettle-hat on his funnel."

> (Shrieks of joy.) I whistle and chuff. Everyone be-
> gins to join in. We speed up; we find time-beat to-
> gether, rhythm together, we are all engines together,
> though I personally do not move except in spirit.
> The children bang into each other a bit. I do not
> criticise *anything.*

Self (thinking of tidiness-training and watching carefully for signs of tiredness. When their creation is
dying a little—we must watch very carefully for this—I
say): "*Into* the station we go. [Noise ceases.] I must rest

a little for the passengers to get out. Then off I go tidily backwards to bed."

Noise starts. I suggest backwards because they are a little out of breath, and they have to go more slowly that way. I say "I" because each child is absorbed now; each of us *is* "I". We must observe, and know how to watch for this moment. Knowing only comes by experience.

Self: "There I am. [Noise ceases.] I'm very tired. So what shall I do?"

Child: "Go ter sleep."

Another: "Undress."

Self: "Yes, I take off my kettle-hat and put it away carefully. . . ."

A giggle or two perhaps, but most are now quiet and intent. I leave time for miming to go on. At this point a child *must not be hurried*. Creation is taking place. I would wait the whole of the rest of the period, if necessary, and suggest nothing except to say "good" at the end of it. But today creation is beginning to fade. There is only one right moment, and I try to catch it.

Self: ". . . And take my wheels off and put them ready for cleaning."

Mime starts up again. If the imaginative suggestion has not met with approval, as being too unreal, there may be hesitation. I notice who hesitates. Is this one mentally older or merely unimaginative? I shall learn *much* about him or her in time, and it will be the greatest aid to me in introducing *all other subjects at school*.

Self: "Undress—mustn't forget to wash—and clean my teeth [etc.]. At last I'm ready for bed [children may begin to lie down]—I'm very tired. Oh dear, I think—I'm going to—sleep."

The children are now all relaxed; some yawn. The mood and atmosphere of voice are important. I judge that that is enough and go to the piano and strike up a march, or put on a record. All children get up eagerly.

Self: "What's this? Is this nice?"

Some children: "Yes."

Self: "Who are you?"

"You" again, not "I", because I notice absorption has gone. They are very young.

Child: "King."

Another: "Soldier."

I accept all suggestions, and make others. We are horses, animals, motors, everything. Immense experience is gained, many parts are tried, all is joy. I never say "do that" in a strong way. *Reason:* A child might not obey. If there are no orders, there can be no disobedience. I avoid a false position. It is always "I am", "you are", *fait accompli*—or "shall we?" Yet there is complete control. They are controlled by friendship, not me, by trust, by joy. They in fact learn to discipline themselves.

Up to seven years old there is quite a need for suggestion in *what* to do, but never show them *how* to do it. That would destroy creation.

Note: Piano *accompanying* movement aids creation. The discipline of a gramophone record *followed* by the children aids control.

Do not be discouraged if at first you do not know when to do all these things, but no doubt you will understand the main outline.

I would do similar things week after week, but, in order to cement the bond of friendship and to offer creative opportunity, I would slowly begin to build stories such as may arise from *their* suggestions.

Example 2—Five to Six Years

The teacher is beating a drum and the children run in. She brings the sound up to a climax when the children are all happily dashing round in a filled-in circle. One last bang and they all stop.

Teacher: "Sit down quietly. Now listen."

> She pings a bit of metal on a string with a nail. It is a very quiet noise and they have to keep quiet to listen.

Teacher: "What does it remind you of? Listen again—now!"

A child: "Mouse."

Another: "Little man."

> There is a box of noises in the corner.

Teacher: "Go and get a noise you like, Jane. Peter, you get one."

> They are sent separately and come back separately in case there is too long a discussion at the box. Each teacher must judge such moments. Jane now has a tambourine, Peter a sort of metal scraper.

Teacher: "Lovely. Now—a little man with big, big feet lived in a castle and he had a little tame mouse he loved very much——"

> (Both ideas from the first answer have been used, even though difficult to fit.)

—"but there was a big and naughty kangaroo who lived outside. You show us the noise the kangaroo makes, Jane. [Jane bumps her tambourine.] You show us the noise the little mouse makes, Peter. [Peter makes scraping noises.] There. Now, stand up everybody and join in the story if you want to. The little man with the big feet is walking about in his castle——"

(By using a tiny sound for big feet the children are helped to find how to make big moves without too much noise. All the children are the little man.)

—"and his little mouse scratches to get in. [Peter makes scraping noises whilst everyone else is a mouse.] The little man takes him by the hand and they go for a walk [ping, ping, ping, goes the teacher]. Suddenly the big kangaroo comes along, bounding over the garden. [Jane makes bounding noises whilst all the rest are kangaroos.] But the little man and the mouse run off just in time [teacher builds up climax on a tambour— all the children run round the room away from an imaginary kangaroo]. He closes the door with a bang. You make the bang. [Some children call "bang", some stamp their feet.] Don't forget to wipe your feet on the mat. Then sit down quietly in front of your fire. Very quiet; that's right. Let's sit quite silent watching the flames for a bit."

This story is quite long enough to begin with. If they have run and been absorbed, they have done a lot. Long stories break down concentration at this age, and are one cause of getting children into habits of not paying proper attention. Short stories are easier to live a little more deeply, and, in using them, habits of concentration for other school subjects are more likely to become established.

Example 3—Six to Seven Years

After about six years of age children may have what I have called *the dawn of seriousness*. Those who have are ready to be cast in small parts. But there is an in-between stage, and we can fill this in by *group* casting. The following is an extract from a report:

Story: ". . . and the banana didn't want to be caught by the policeman at all, and he ran away. But a motor-car came bundling along towards him. He stopped for a moment, and then the policeman caught him. The policeman stopped the car, he and the banana got in, and the driver took them to the prison. The banana was put safely behind bars and carefully locked up, and couldn't be naughty again."

In this case, one child, who was ready for casting, was the policeman, two children were the man who drove the car; the car was four children, but the banana was five children. They were not all linked together physically, making one big banana, but were five separate entities linked emotionally, and so giving each other the group courage to dare that colossal act—being a banana. (See Diagram A.)

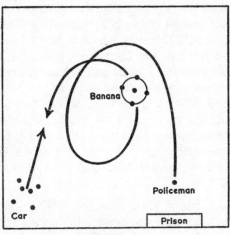

Diagram A

Example 4

Self (softly rubbing together two pieces of sandpaper):
    "What does this sound remind you of?"

Child: "Cat scratching."

Self (tapping tambour with a stick): "And this one?"

Child: "Man running."

Self (stamping on a rostrum block): "And this?"
        No answer.

Self: "Well, it reminds me of—say, a door banging?"

Child: "Yes."

Another: "Or a tyre bursting."

Self (delighted): "Yes! Now let's make a story out of these
    ideas."

> "A man was walking down a passage in a big, big
> house, when suddenly he heard a funny noise. He
> thought it might be burglars, and he started to run.
> But when he got to the end of the passage he found
> it was only his cat scratching the door of a room, be-
> cause he was shut out. So the man opened the door,
> the cat rushed through it, dashed to a window and
> jumped out. The man ran after him to see what had
> happened, but just then there was a big bang. The
> door of the room had slammed shut again in the wind.
> But something else had happened, too: the cat had
> jumped right on to the back of a motor-car standing
> outside the house, and do you know his claws were
> *so out* and *ready* to catch at something, that they'd
> gone right through the spare tyre at the back of the
> car when he landed there, and the tyre was as flat as
> a fish."

The story would then be acted. "Who would like to
be . . ." etc. I would accompany the acting with sounds,
e.g. tambour for man running. The car would be made of

several people and would no doubt collapse if the cat jumped off a chair on to it. Some children would be wind, others furniture in the passage, two or three the door. There might be many cars, many men, but slowly such attempts become more like a cast play as children approach six and seven years.

Because the children are suggesting the ideas that lead to the story, they are already sharing in part of the creation.

Note.—"Now let's make a story. . . ." We're all doing this together. It's not just me telling a story. Later, they will be able to share in the creation even more fully. For instance, one of the ideas may be left out, or you may suddenly stop and say something like: "And what do you think happened then?" or "Who do you think they saw rushing along the road?" Such opportunities to join in are readily accepted by the children after only a little experience of this work. Teachers who are worried by feelings that they are unable to make up stories easily should take confidence from this. Ultimately, the children will be able to make up some stories entirely on their own, but until then they will often help us if we run out of ideas.

The above are some suggestions for ways of beginning in the infant school. Be content with small beginnings, for the small things are really great. You will have done a magnificent job if, by the time the children have reached six and a half years, they have discovered the full significance of time-beat and rhythm, and their difference: if the older children do not bump into each other, and equidistance has begun to appear during play; if they have learned to love sound; if you occasionally get good contrasts and climaxes; if you have achieved "pin drop" control; and if absorption and sincerity have been developed.

Remember that you are part of a team in your school and that it is important to use many quiet moments in play of this kind which give children a deeper aesthetic experience and help them to understand discipline. Always finish such a period with some quiet suggestion. E.g.

Teacher (tapping a tambour very quietly): "I want to hear the clock ticking, so go out very quietly to your next class."

This has been *personal* play; they must be prepared for the *projected* play of other studies.

You will help the work and the children if, in the infant school, you try to avoid all playing to parents, use of formal stage and script plays, and use only a little dressing-up. These things interfere with the absorption, and thus the sincerity, if they are experienced too soon.

Language Flow

There may be some flow of spontaneous language by six years, and, though movement is an important form of language at this age, spontaneous speech cannot start too early. They learn to use and love language, and the sounds bring recognition musically. Language contains vowels and consonants. Sounds are roughly divided into elongated sounds and short, sharp ones. Strings, bells and gongs offer us long sounds, unless specially arranged otherwise. Sharp sounds come from percussion instruments, tapping and banging things, though of course there are intermediate sounds, too. By carefully nurtured love, first of sound itself and then of special sounds—short and sharp, then of sounds containing mood—it is possible to associate sound of many kinds (starting with the vowels and consonants) with language in general. The child then transfers its love to speech. Parallel with this should come spontaneous play where speech enters. Practice in speaking creatively and learning the love of sound is the best approach to language.

Here are some actual examples of spontaneous speech stimulated by these methods—it nearly always has poetic or philosophic content for children over six, and often religious thought, too:

Girl (6): "Look! There is my own dear friend the first evening star."

Girl (6½): "And the warm came, and the rain came, and the sad, sad clouds. Then I knew it was time for bed."

Girl (7) (dancing all over the room): "I am joy-riding over the sun on a bright nail."

Boy (6½): "And I got me gun and I lifted it, and the angel came out of the sun and I threw it away."

Boy (7) (as the good Samaritan, turning over the wounded man and saying *very* tenderly): " 'Oo done it?"

Working under Difficulties

If you have little space and only a classroom to work in, try to arrange to move the desks. If this is not possible, do what you can and *use* the desks. Turn them into mountains, ships, horses or cowsheds. A certain amount of movement can take place amongst them. Use noises here also. If only a few can act at a time, encourage audience participation. Fight against the shape of the rigid theatre with actors' end (teacher's end) and audience end (pupils' end). If actors turn their backs on the other actors who sit and participate in their desks, do not on any account correct this. The actors who have more movement than the others are merely forming part of the circle, normal at this age, which we would see in its entirety under better conditions. Remember in Child Drama there is no real audience, and take comfort from the fact that, by your kindly sympathy, children will get much more than you think out of the worst possible conditions, because of their wonderful imagination. They need opportunity, that is all.

Common both to the best conditions and the less good is the task of the teacher in acting as a kindly and gentle guide. Encouragement is needed at this age, and some stimulation. If speech or play fails at a certain moment, learn to be sensitive about when to make a suggestion and what suggestion, and when *not* to. This is the art of nurturing.

CHAPTER IV

WHAT TO DO WITH JUNIORS

Seven to Nine Years

Continue with much the same kind of work as in an infant school, but encourage rather longer scenes, give less direction in what to do (still avoiding telling or showing how to do it), use longer and more complicated stories and cast more often. Here is a further example of *The Ideas Game* method of reaching a story, this time without the use of sounds to stimulate the ideas. (This method would be of great value with junior children who have done none of this work in their infant schools.)

Example of Work taken in a School

Self: "Let's have some ideas."
A child: "A river."
Another: "Little boy."
Another: "Willow tree."
Another: "Horrid mother."
Self: "Right, here's our story, then:

"Once upon a time there was a *little boy* who had a *horrid mother*. She beat him, she starved him and made him work half the night. He never got any sweets, not even any bubble gum. And they lived by a thin silver *river*, the colour of the moon. One night, the little boy looked out of the window, and as he looked the moon was reflected in the river and he saw quite clearly the man in the moon. Whether it was the movement of the water or not the little boy didn't know, but all at once he saw the

Moon-Man's mouth move and heard a voice saying:
'Don't stay, little boy, come out and live by the river.'
Then a cloud came and the moon disappeared. The little
boy threw on some clothes, took his favourite bit of
string and a bright button from under his pillow, and
crept downstairs and out of the house. Once outside, he
ran as fast as he could until he dropped exhausted by the
river bank and went to sleep. In his sleep he dreamt that a
willow tree bent over him and hummed a leafy song. The
tree sang: 'I will be your mother. If ever you want
strength, suck the green twig I hold towards you and
everything will be all right.'

"The little boy woke up and there, sure enough, was the
willow tree, waving and waiting. He sucked one of the
green fingers. A flood of happiness leapt up in him, and a
taste of electric honey. He ran and ran, with the dew in
his hair and an early sun shining through it. Suddenly he
saw a farm, and the farmer gave him some wood to chop,
and food for doing it. But the little boy never would stay
with the farmer and his kind wife. He always went back
to the willow, his new mother. Whenever he needed
strength, he sucked the green twig. And he grew and grew
and became the strongest wood-chopper in the whole
district. But one day the river got angry and began to
break its banks. He didn't know why, but the little boy,
who was now quite a big boy, you remember, thought of
his real mother. With a loud bang, part of the bank broke
and the water began to pour through. The boy started to
dash towards his old home and arrived just in time to save
his mother. They made a raft of an old door and paddled
towards the kind farmer. By the time they arrived safely
at the high ground of the farm, the old mother had re-
pented of her unkindness and the boy forgave her. They
all lived at the farm, and the kind farmer's wife taught

Juniors at Rea Street Drama Centre, Birmingham

Juniors at Rea Street Drama Centre: Rhythmic head chopping.
Good absorption and believable situation

Junior school: The Sermon on the Mount

Senior boys—lower school: Robin Hood and his men attack from high ground. Note flow off stage (see p. 59)

the mother how to stay kind all the time—a jolly difficult thing to do. But, do you know, when the river had gone back into the long bed of its banks, the willow tree had entirely disappeared. Wasn't that extraordinary? Sometimes the Moon-Man seemed to appear in the river and to wobble his mouth about, but for some reason that cannot be understood he never spoke again."

A child: "Why did the river get angry?"

Self: "I don't know. What do you think?"

Another child: "'E got angry wiv the mother 'cos she'd done somethink 'orrible."

Another child: "The man in the moon said something 'e didn't like."

Self: "Yes, there might have been all sorts of reasons. Now, when we come to that bit (all who would like to), think what would make *you* angry if you were the river. Then the river will get angry all right. The boy's house is over there. Let's have the river here. Make a nice pattern with it. Where will the tree be?" (They told me. I just wanted to give them enough of the geography for the essentials to be clear. They suggested the rest and chose the cast.)

A child: "Can we 'ave the table for the house?"

Self: "Yes, and the rest of it can be you three." (I suggested this because three children obviously wanted to join the group but hadn't been invited yet. They made themselves into gables. But ten or fifteen children were still on one side of the room, and about eight on the other.)

Self: "You ten be animals on the farm. The rest of you be the river."

I didn't have to say any more. They organised all the rest. I just suggested when it should begin. Everyone joined in to make the special "leafy humming" of the willow tree. Children who were being the river lay down in a curly line and got up in a swarm to overflow the banks. We used part of a record of the music of *Job* to accompany this. My task was to fade it in on the gramophone to provide an inspiring background. The story took twenty-four minutes to play through. (See Diagram B.)

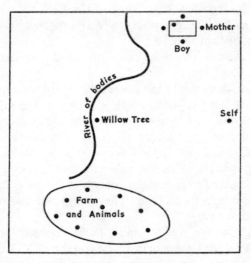

Diagram B

Polishing Improvisations

Allow more repetition of the play themes and occasionally polish the improvised attempts by putting in suggestions. So that their enthusiasm is not dampened, let them play through first and then discuss afterwards.

Example

"Yes, I like the way you did that. Do you think we could make it [NOT—you'd be better if] more interesting and exciting?"

Accept their answers. Use their suggestions, if any, and add something of your own like: "I thought it would be better if the messenger came in more excited still, in more of a rush, then the people chasing him could rush in, too; but instead of getting into a bundle near that part of the room they could use the space in this part, fill it in and make a nice shape." I don't tell them at this age what shape to make, merely draw attention to some little piece of beauty they may have missed. They do it—not me.

This one suggestion may be quite enough to give added life to the whole theme. Few suggestions, but carefully chosen ones, are right. Too many suggestions depress them. We must be very careful not to interfere or nag.

I hope this advice may aid those who are afraid direction will kill creation, and, on the other hand, give encouragement to those who are convinced that the sympathetic adult has an important contribution to make when present during dramatic play in school. These moments are education as differentiated from playing in the playground. Children do not come to school for nothing. But it is wise to accept their way of going about things, and it is not dishonest to avail oneself of opportunities of building wisdom and finding achievement together.

Language Flow

Towards nine years, children are well able to invent and act stories of their own, though dialogue becomes more earthy and wit is quicker. Here is an extract from the dialogue of one of these creations:

Boy (as factory owner, to spiv trying to get a job): "Owja get inter my faktry with them wide shoulders? The door's too narrah."

Spiv (quick as lightning): "Ah, I coom in sidewiz."

We get genuine dialect and a flow of language often coming straight out of home background at this age.

Outbursts of speech, creative or otherwise, are greatly to be encouraged. It is important that there should be practice. You need not fear that frank and open children will be impudent; on the whole they are not, and by winning their friendship and trust one is ultimately rewarded by their trying to be pleasant and helpful. But this entirely depends on whether the adult honestly treats the child as a decent human being or as something inferior.

Dialect is primarily a question of music, and the ear becoming used to certain sounds. Though we may love good speech, it is very important not to make children feel ashamed of the music of their home background. To force an artificial change of personal music may sever many ties and produce a fish out of water. Artificial, half-improved speech is a joy to no one. It is much better to let the dialect remain, but encourage some habits of clarity. At the same time it is perfectly possible to give the child the idea of turning on the tap of another kind of speech, which should not be presented as *better* but *different*. Most children are very adaptable in this way and can turn on the tap quite easily, and, if encouraged in the right manner, are quick to discover the occasions when the different types of language are appropriate. For instance, it is common for children to speak reasonably well and quietly in school and to be loud and unintelligible in the street. But it is interesting to note that where good opportunity for language flow is given *in* school, rowdiness outside diminishes. This does not happen if formal training is the only training received, for one of the causes of stridency is lack of opportunity for outburst. There *will* be outbursts somewhere and somehow; we might just as well ensure that they are legitimate, intended, creative and beautiful.

We also get apparently incongruous and anachronistic pieces of life experience being brought in. For instance, a particularly holy band of monks I once met would burst out suddenly singing "Roll out the barrel" at regular intervals. But, after all, there is a sort of logic about this.

Here is an example of inventive dialogue:

Girl (8): "I am the man with the electric nose. I speak and spark like the sun, and the wicked ones fear my sparking as I come. I fear it, too, but I don't tell anyone."

Acting Out

When they make up their own plays, allow lots of playing out of characters and themes of which you may disapprove. In this way family and personal worries are eased and the results of seeing anti-social films and hearing violent radio may be worked off. We must not forget that at such moments children are sharing an important personal secret with us; it is a confession; they find relief in our friendship which allows them to play out illegal acts in a legalised manner. We should not shut them up nor rebuff them.

It should be noted that therapeutic playing out of this

simple nature is largely unconscious (though intentional cartooning may be contained in it) for the younger child, and it is a mistake to impose, too suddenly, conscious problems to enact. This is very important for the consideration of those concerned with maladjusted and emotionally disturbed children.

This type of play is a form of spitting out, and can be changed gradually to stories of more savoury character, if adult judgment is unbiased and the right moment chosen for making suggestions.

Example

By careful judgment and a little tactful shepherding, it is possible for a gangster to end up as Christopher Columbus —which is wonderful, because Christopher Columbus is history and therefore respectable.

It would happen through discussion:

"All right; well, we've had a lot of good gangster work. Now let's change the theme a little and have our gangsters in a boat. Anybody know anything about pirates? What do they wear? Who has to deal with smugglers? Anyone know?"

So we work towards considering coastguards; let them play a theme on that, and then follow with some such words:

"It must have been awful in the days when you couldn't put out to sea without being afraid of pirates. Do you know the names of any people who might have found it difficult to put out to sea? Not necessarily anyone who was afraid, but someone who would have to think twice about pirates? Anyone know the names of people in history who would have had to cope with this?"

If no one answers, supply a name. Have a voyage of discovery. Associate the rough behaviour of the original gangsters with a more constructive purpose; let them be explorers and savages with vigour, but, if you wish to ensure some moral instruction, see that at one time they understand that the good man can win. I always have one period dropping the hint that there can be such a thing as a good coastguard, and a good pirate, and that mercy rather than death, and justice rather than law, are important. It helps them to understand authority in school without resentment.

The playing out has a markedly improving effect upon behaviour, and can act as a simple form of prevention of neurosis. It is only a slight exaggeration to say that the clinic has to patch up by play methods what our education has failed to prevent.[1] Wouldn't it be more sensible to have this simpler form of prevention established on a much wider scale in education? (I'm sure it will be, one day.)

Do not let anyone be disturbed by this reference to therapy. Much of it is a perfectly natural process, and, in any case, it is very important not to stifle a healthy interest in adventure. This is a virile side of youth, a potential part of a virile nation; it only needs guiding aright.

In the chapter devoted to this subject in the main book, *Child Drama*, Dr. William Kraemer, formerly Deputy Director of the Davidson Clinic, Edinburgh, and now working in London, is quoted as saying:

[1] See also *Dramatherapy as an aid to Personal Development*, published by the Guild of Pastoral Psychology, 25 Porchester Terrace, London W.

"I find myself in complete agreement with Peter Slade's ideas on drama. I have heard a good deal of his work and seen some, and I feel sure that drama as conceived by him will prove of great value to education and therapy of society and the individual. Slade rightly emphasises the role drama should play in the prevention of neurosis. I fully agree. There have been many cases under my observation in which drama has had a curative effect in neurotic illnesses, and sometimes it has been of the greatest importance. There is hardly a patient who does not in one way or another find in his artistic expression the highroad to health. It may be drawing or painting, music or poetry . . . it is always a creative activity, it is always drama in Slade's definition of it as creative 'doing'."

Rostrum Blocks

Still use only the floor space in the junior school. If a stage exists in the hall, use it only as a simple location such as a palace. The world is the floor of the hall, where most of the action should take place in the development of genuine Child Drama.

However, do make use of rostrum blocks. They can be used in projected play, as a development of nursery bricks with which to build things, and in personal play as a means of developing a sense of music, rhythm and dramatic climax, and also for beginning to sense the effect of being raised up. I discovered this through studying the enormous empire of street play. There exists in street play a discovery of higher levels, because of the kerbstones and pavements contrasting with the road. Amongst many rhythmic adventures causing delight, I distinguished in running play the climax. This takes place when emotional music of the feet carries the child on to the pavement. The higher level in itself appears to be a stimulus and is clearly used with conscious satisfaction. I intend that as many children as possible shall have the opportunity of discovering this joy *in* school, where it can be even more constructive and is without danger to life.

Running play itself appears to be an expression of sheer joy accompanied generally by bent knees, arms wide and ecstatic expression. It only grows in a happy atmosphere, and I have never seen it in any junior school where a stage is extensively used and formal theatre with scripts takes place.

The use of the higher level provided by rostrum blocks is also a slow approach to the use of a stage.[1] Any sudden use of a stage brings showing off, which is as injurious to the developing personality as it is to the drama itself.

Nine to Eleven Years

Between the years of nine and eleven, when play has become established, the adult has the opportunity of adding further to their creations. It does not in any way destroy their best work to suggest themes coming from the myths and legends of the world. It helps us to introduce them to literature. They will have become familiar with some of these stories already in reading lessons, and by using them we give an opportunity for more complicated characterisations and situations, and the possibility of developing a deeper sense of plot and form. Some of these can be repeated and dressed, and, as long as freshness is carefully guarded, can give us remarkable glimpses of their art, Child Drama, now coming nearer to theatre.

Script-plays are not advocated at all for the junior school, so that even in this type of creation we use the

[1] See also *School Stages*, a pamphlet published by the Educational Drama Association.

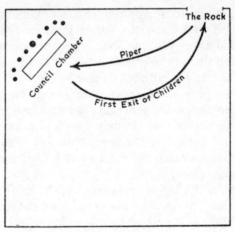

Diagram C1

story only as a theme for spontaneous expression, and the movement may travel all over the room. But we polish.

Example (see Diagrams C1 and C2)

This school was beginning an improvisation on the oft-used *Pied Piper of Hamelin*. It was going fairly well in places, but was rather unimaginative. The teacher intended polishing it a bit, but it wasn't improving.

Teacher (to me): "What would you do to get it better?"

Self: "Well, first of all, try letting the whole thing open with the Pied Piper dancing alone—perhaps practising his special fairy piece. I always wonder where on earth he got that charm in his music from. You might discuss that one time. The children will probably give you good ideas for a whole new beginning to this story, which we grown-ups know so well! What we don't know is—was it the piper or the tune which put a spell on the rats and children? At least, I don't know. But, about what I've

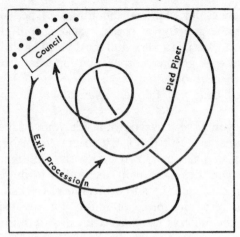

Diagram C2

just seen: the town councillors are not alive yet. The mayor needs more character. Is he weak or a bully? The movement round, when they go after the piper, is dull. Let them use a big sweep all over the floor of the hall. There might be slow drum-beats to accompany the slow steps when the piper approaches the guilty town council. Make it more atmospheric. If no one can play a pipe, fade in some fairy music on the gramophone for the march round, and be sure you lift the playing head straight off as the rock closes suddenly behind the children. In the quiet moment left by the sudden cutting-off of music we shall be touched the more deeply by the lonely rhythmic tap of the cripple's crutch. Couldn't there be special rat music, too? Or discuss with the children what noises could be made by shaking things or making rattles for the scurrying noise. I think the mayor might have a proper feast, too. There ought to be crabs, candles, buns, ices, sea serpents, comics for napkins, mountains of pop bottles, noises of the popping of corks, crackers, and clinking noises for forks. It's a very dull meal yet. I can't believe the mayor ever got his 'corporation' on what you have allowed them to do so far."

Teacher: "Oh dear, yes, I do see. I haven't got the imagination."

Self: "Yes, you have. Deep down inside yourself it's waiting to come out. But don't try to create all by yourself. Discuss much more often with the children. They will give you ideas and help your mind to flow. Your task with this age is to add a little form to their work, like that very nice piece of music you are using to build up the finish of the play. They are all in time and there is a good strong exit. Really well done."

Teacher: "Oh, I'm glad I've got something right."

Self: "You've got a lot right. Courage. Go on. You are doing well. It is not easy to leap into a new world, but we can ooze ourselves in by finding more and more of what is in the child's mind. There is always something. We must find it."

Teacher: "Would you take on for a bit?"

Self: "I'll just try to release them a little if you like."

I then discussed with the children what would be the best feast in the world, hoping the teacher would take note. After having a good imaginary blow-out, they all became fat rats and danced to a rhumba record (appropriate somehow for heavy-tummied creatures). After talking about what real fairy music in this situation would be like, we finished up with a mighty procession of all the councillors, rats and children in the world being friendly together, marching as one in large figure-of-eight shapes about the whole floor, to the glowing strains of the ballet *Sylvia*. Speech had come much more freely, absorption had improved and the acting was much more virile and believable. Later, I heard that a witch finally told the piper what music to use, and a goblin riding on a camel took telegrams from the piper to the town council.

Group Sensitivity and Child Dance

After nine years of age it is possible during child-created dance to develop a group sensitivity. They feel and dance together at these moments, and there is no bumping whatever. The circles of the gang[1] disappear and equidistance is marked. There is one whole sensitive group dancing in accord. I am personally convinced that this is a social experience of the greatest magnitude, and that those who leave school without it have lost an important gift both to themselves and to the community.

The dance itself can become extremely well developed between seven and twelve years of age, where opportunity is given for it. By nine or ten we may expect to see intense imaginative work of either a flowing or a stylised kind. It can be ethereal or broadly comic. It can be of the gang (a few children dancing together) or of the whole community (all the class). Dances, as with plays, may be creations partly of the child, partly of the teacher; often the children make the whole thing themselves. Great attention is paid to the sound of feet and to space relationships. The intense beauty of the work is in the shapes drawn, as it were, by the path of movement over the floor space, and in the ever-changing groups. Absorption and sincerity are the core of the work, and its outer mastery is the use of space.

One of the important things about genuine Child Dance is that it helps to develop an individual style of movement. The individual style in dance is as important as style in

[1] The gang groups usually are made up of from five to seven children.

handwriting. You might say that these are the two sides
of expression again, personal and projected play. They
are bound up with personality, and this is the secret of the
profound effect of dance. This suggestion that there exists
an individual style will give rise to many questions about
the desirability of imposing specialised forms of movement
too early.

There also comes a time between nine and eleven,
which I look out for with interest: during play on the
floor the child stops and consciously takes in his neigh-
bour, and the player beyond that and beyond again. It is
what Spengler in another context has called "depth consciousness", which is linked later with ability to use
perspective in Child Art.

Try to help the child to find this in actual three dimen-
sions during dance. It affects painting, and makes conse-
quent technical discovery of perspective less of a problem.
Child Drama, with wider recognition, may one day add
much knowledge to what has always been something of an
enigma in this process. I have merely discovered that these
things are so, and that Child Drama eases and enriches
Child Art in numerous ways.

By eleven years of age there should be extreme sincerity and absorption during play, much beautiful movement, and a healthy, easy flow of spontaneous speech,
which compared with a learnt script is as life against
death. Do not write plays for them or use other scripted
plays. Their own attempts at script plays are disappointing, too. The junior child has not the facility for writing
dialogue, though he is well able to speak it. The result, in
comparison, is disappointing, and hours of their labour
will produce a poor little vehicle which is played through
in a couple of minutes. It is much better to encourage
them to write a story about what happens in their play.

They will have success in this, and you will find occasionally that direct statements are included in the story. This is the beginning of dialogue.

Costume

Though children of this age take great delight in dressing-up, their grace and beauty of movement are still somewhat hindered by clothes. Where the work and conditions as described do not obtain, more use is made of clothes, but where the child's own drama is allowed and understood we find more pleasure in the actual drama itself, and children by their own wish may use only very little clothing, or discard it altogether. The adult should take care not to burden the child with dress, for this bewilders it. From the creative point of view pieces of attractive stuff are better than ready-made garments, as children can continue to create with these, building up a true character with costume to match. An over-elaborate costume often over-balances the creation, and true characterisation decreases because of interest in parading up and down. This, in turn, tends to more showing off, and eventual deterioration in perhaps the whole period of work.

The creative use of bits and pieces also has valuable lessons in the sphere of choice and taste, with a whole range of most interesting creative needlework; bits of paper or objects may be sewn or stuck on to coloured stuffs. But the fuller version of this task is so absorbing that it is best done separately. Again, the final costume (which is better than that of ready-made garments) is often too greatly loved, admired and cared for to be a useful aid to good drama. It is used for a careful absorbed parading, which is rather more a personal fulfilment of the process of art creation, and is only drama of the less obvious kind. On the other hand, the quicker, simple creation is definitely intended as an aid to drama. The wearing of "uncreated" garments is seldom art or drama; there is usually a motive behind it, often linked with the adult, and generally bad.

Working under Difficulties

If you have to use classrooms, move the desks. If there are sufficient reasons for not doing that, consider complete and permanent change of shape so as to allow more space in the centre. It will aid all teaching. The same number of desks may fit on three sides or in a semi-circle. Otherwise use the desks themselves, as you would for occasional finding of a higher level with rostrum blocks.

Do everything you can to avoid suggesting actor and audience as different. Do not encourage a narrator, who breaks up the scenes and talks to an audience. Encourage audience participation if some have to sit in desks. Do not stop actors turning their backs. We are not in the theatre. What is taking place is much more important. It is life in the making. There may be small circles in cramped space, or a half-circle against the back wall. Encourage play between the desks, also, if in rows with aisles.

The existence of the gang makes splitting up into smaller playing groups a fairly natural process in the junior school, but do not yet encourage actor and audience differences or you will get showing-off. The classroom is a perfectly reasonable place, though, for short playlets created by children and acted by groups in succession. Though space is lacking, much else is gained. Encourage language flow. If it has had a fair chance and a clear run from the infant school up, it will be good by now. Don't stop improvised speech because you can't put up with it, or don't see the point of it. You don't stop practice in

Senior boys: The Sheriff's men overcome the outlaws. Law and order triumphs. Note grace and agility of imaginary sword play on right (see pp. 68–70)

Young class of Secondary Modern boys: This is a motor-coach. People are taught how to travel from place to place by bus also; how to put their luggage on the rack without knocking their neighbours' hats off; and eventually they will be taught not to stand on the seat!

Beginning improvised dance with Senior girls at Rea Street Drama Centre, Birmingham: Note climax in use of rostrum block

Senior girls: Really good group work. Space is well filled and grace developing

writing because you are bored with children's essays. Do not stop practice in speech.

With juniors, as with infants, the teacher's main task is that of acting as a kindly, gentle guide. But in the junior school more polish is needed occasionally when you do enter into things. However, responsibility for good creation should be handed more and more to the child, until with the older ones it is almost entirely handed over; together with this goes responsibility for good behaviour. This is the way to help parents and in part avoid delinquency. Successful Child Drama in the junior school is not only education at its highest, but prevention also. It provides a legitimate outlet for the atom-bomb energy of that social group we call the gang.

CHAPTER V

WHAT TO DO WITH SENIORS

Eleven to Thirteen Years Old (Experienced Children)

IT is seldom necessary to give many suggestions at this age to children at all experienced in Child Drama. Ideas flow, though it is still necessary to watch carefully, and to encourage those that appear shy, for this is the age when self-consciousness may develop. We can prevent it from doing so.

Continue in the secondary modern school as in the junior school. For at least the first year allow, encourage and expect play on the floor. Themes normally will be fuller and accomplishment more polished (though sometimes there is a trace of younger ideas because of emotional upset due to change of school), but outward shape of behaviour on the floorspace will often be the same, even though shape in painting may have begun to grope towards the future. For many children the peak period of acting in a manner which does not include the proscenium stage continues after eleven years old; also the consciousness and understanding of depth may not have any pronounced manifestations in outward forms of play until about thirteen years. Have in mind that there may be gradual advance over the floorspace towards the stage, or at least to play which takes place at one end of a room. With first-year children, keep the curtains of the stage shut (if you have any). This reduces the overwhelming influence of the stage upon their work. Any move towards using it is then likely to become a genuine inner urge towards new forms of expression and discovery.

For Beginners

If they are inexperienced, start, as with younger children, building a story or situation out of ideas pieced together between the children and yourself; these will of course be "older" in thought by now than those given in the junior examples.

Example—Someone has suggested a station:

Teacher: "What sort of people appear on a station?"

At infant level the answers expected would be "train", "man with flag", etc. Here, with young seniors, they are:

A tired old lady;
An angry passenger in a hurry who has lost his ticket;
A frightened dog.

We can aid them to more sense of character and situation and observation of the daily drama of life.

The whole classroom or hall may then be turned into a station; later, when some practice at being these people has been experienced, a simple situation might be introduced by, for example, someone snatching a lady's handbag, or the frightened dog barking at an old man, etc. These early scenes may be quite short, but can be taken in fairly rapid succession. Keep things going so that the scene does not die.

If left alone, boys often play gangster themes or space themes, and girls such themes as hat shops. But even hat shops may be led away to a consideration of how you serve politely behind a counter.

Example—Twelve to Thirteen Years (Girls)

From a school visit:

They had been improvising a hat shop scene for some

time on the floor of the hall in front of the stage. But their imagination had been failing a little and play petered out.

Self: "Did you think the girls serving were very kind to the old gentleman buying his wife a hat?"

Girls: "No."

Self: "I know this was just your own acting, but should we try again now, and think carefully about how to serve well and consider the customer?"

>We began again. The girls behind the counter talked. The customer waited.

Self: "It's better to pay attention to the customer straight away. Wouldn't it be kinder to offer the old people a chair, too?"

>We began again. They were much more considerate.

Self: "Good. That's much better. I wouldn't mind going into that hat shop. Just one point. Did you notice that the girl who went off to get a bonnet for the old lady pulled a face at the other girl? Now if you were really the old lady, what would you feel?"

Answers: "Be angry." "Be upset." "Walk out, I should."

Self: "Yes, you might do any of those things. I don't think we realise often enough that when we deal in shops, banks, buses and offices, we really *are* serving the public. People have an absolute right to expect thoughtfulness and good manners. It is much better for business, too. You sell more that way."

>We tried out several groups of buyers and sellers. Improvement came rapidly.

Self: "Now, before next time I want you to think very hard about this, and next week you can show your teacher the best run, most polite hat shop in the world. And I bet it will be good." (See Diagram D.)

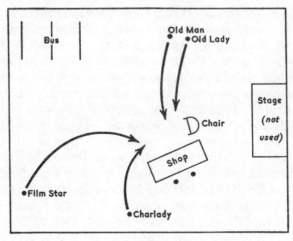

Diagram D

How to Bridge the Gap between Improvisation and Script Plays

At about thirteen years expect to find a desire for script plays creeping in. The first step towards this is improvisation, after which the teacher writes down certain sentences selected and agreed by the group to be the best; then repetition of that improvised piece with the written-down parts kept in, though the rest may change slightly. Repeat this, but with more discussion afterwards to see if further improvement can be made on the dialogue, being careful not to make anyone feel he has done badly. Don't say things like: "No, no, that won't do; he wouldn't say that"; but encourage with such remarks as: "I wonder if that man in that situation would really say that? Do you think perhaps he might be a little more frightened or excited?" You thus obtain confidence and interest for group suggestion and group agreement on the improvement of the lines. Quite a lot of script now exists. The rest is still left to improvisation. Final stage—discussion, with or without improvised play, round some theme to do with the school, or to do with some simple problem in life, or something exciting that happened in the newspapers. Here the complete script is evolved and written, and may be learnt if thought appropriate. Children may be encouraged after such experiences as these to write their own plays, having picked up some notions of effective dialogue, plot, form and length of scene. Do not necessarily cramp their efforts by putting these on to a stage; it is better at first to feel and play in the shape appropriate to the situation, which may be on the floor of the hall.

After this, they may be ready for plays written by other people. But do not allow undue regard for your own love of *good literature* to force the pace. All comes better if slowly and organically evolved; also, an adolescent is still searching for the true self. Simple plays offering strong characterisation are often more important than "good stuff". We are educating individuals in this process, not training professional actors. But keep developing their interest in sound and they will begin to "hear" the beauty in literature. This is a much better and more genuine way of arriving at good taste.

Rostrum Blocks

Continue to use rostrum blocks, because by allowing construction of the units you can notice the slow movement of higher levels to one end of a room, indicating emotional and intellectual readiness for the more traditional theatre form. It is now coming because *they* want it, and not because we want it. Only in this way is an artificial domination by the proscenium form of theatre avoided. If and when they ask for a stage, open the curtains and let them use it. I always hope this will not happen too early in a child's life; much is lost by too early an experience of the proscenium stage. Some important link in the realm of depth discovery and the slow appreciation of perspective (see p. 50) may be lost; also opportunities for running play, and for unconscious absorption of the whole history of the theatre and its various shapes.

Note now what happens to art. Expect discovery of the perspective theatre form to be linked with exploration in perspective and questions about it in painting and drawing, if these have not arisen before. Always try to see that there is easy access on and off the stage so that a flow of movement on and off can take place. Children are eminently wise. They are not so vulgar as to try to cram far too many people into far too small a space. They flow on and off when they need to, and take joy in good grouping, undirected and personally sensed. There are no self-consciously "highbrow" productions as such in Child Drama, but a genuine sense of developed taste decides the right form for the right creation. (See photograph opposite page 37.)

Thirteen to Fourteen Years

In general, the script play is taking further hold, and movement is becoming somewhat restricted. We find less flowing *off* the stage. Still hold regular periods of improvisation, though, so that imaginative creation is not sacrificed for an intellectual literary approach.

Also polish improvisations more often.

Example

Here is part of a play made up by boys in a secondary modern school, performed in the classroom. Four boys came running in.

1st boy: "Let's have one last look at the map before we prepare for the journey."

2nd boy: "That's a good idea."

3rd boy: "Cor, someone's been at my haversack."

1st boy: "My haversack's been tampered with as well."

2nd boy: "And mine."

3rd boy: "That means somebody must have stolen it."

2nd boy: "Yes, while we were downstairs. It must have been the keeper."

1st boy: "Yes, he was a conspicuous-looking character, I must say."

4th boy: "Yes, he is."

3rd boy: "He was rather cut up about that little idol . . . what I had."

2nd boy: "He must have known about it."

4th boy: "Well, who could have told him?"

1st boy: "Remember when he came into the room—we had the map out then."

4th boy: "No—we put it away before he came in."

2nd boy: "Yes, that's right."

3rd boy: "He really got his hair up when he saw that little idol and remembered it was attached to the map."

1st boy: "Well, I can't see what the little idol's meant for, I'm sure."

2nd boy: "Nor me."

4th boy: "Well, there's only one person who can have had the map, and that's the keeper."

Here the scene stopped.

Teacher (to self): "Well, so much for that, Mr. Slade. What do you think about it, and do you think it has any possibilities? Are there any points where you think it can be improved upon?"

Self (to teacher): "Yes, I think we can improve upon that now. It wants to be a little louder and a bit more

Secondary Modern girls: Dance drama (see p. 66)

Example of virile dance in a Secondary Modern boys' school (see p. 65)

exciting, and I don't think there's any harm in suggesting that afterwards to boys of their age; one can certainly do that—they're sensible enough to begin to take production now. [To the boys]: That was very nice. I want you to do it again, but this time when you come in, can you try to make it even faster and louder and even more exciting. It doesn't matter how fast you go, but try to think of the excitement building up like a mountain and you'll have got us all absolutely interested and right on our toes. Ready."

Again they run in.

1st boy: "Let's have one last look at the map before we prepare for the journey."

2nd boy: "Yes, that's a good idea."

Self: "Yes, that's not quite good enough yet. Let's try again, shall we? And when you come, move faster, running in. You're in a rage, aren't you?"

The play started again, but was once more stopped at the end of the same passage.

Self: "That's much better. Now, there's just one point before we run it all once again. Do you remember you say: 'Let's have a look at the map' or something, don't you? Let's do it again and make it a strong L on 'Let's'."

The play starts again, but this time it is allowed to run its course without stoppage of any kind. In this way confidence is upheld, and no further suggestion or comment is made until this is fully restored. Note also the manner of handling, which is swift, warm and in keeping with the excitement of the play. This method of polishing an improvisation retains the natural flow and spontaneity, but gives a first introduction to the type of work that will be more essential with script plays.

Fourteen to Fifteen Years

Some polishing is beginning in rehearsal of script plays. But if the rehearsal goes dead I break it up, bring all the players off the stage and improvise the scene on the floor-space until life, confidence and spontaneity have returned.

Reason: This has a marked effect on the continued rehearsal. Life and understanding are added to it.

Example

A master was taking a rehearsal of part of *Noah* (Obey) on the floor of the hall. I stood near. Three out of five players were reading the script with great difficulty and not speaking loud enough. Another group was rehearsing as animals on the stage, together with Mr. Noah. Presently I moved over to them. A mistress was trying to encourage Noah to get into his part more; he was reading with great difficulty.

The teacher (quietly): "*How* do you get them to get inside the part?"

Self: "They never will whilst they are having such difficulty with the scripts. If you want more meaning, which is the first sign of getting more into the part, I should try Noah without the book for a bit. Get him to make up his own words—words that he thinks he would say himself if he were really that person in that situation. That will give him a chance to create. He is chained by his inability to read a script, at the moment. Look at those animals. They are quite different. They are *acting* because they have no scripts. They are free."

The teacher tried this. At first Noah was self-conscious.

Self (quietly to teacher): "Go on. Persevere."

At the third attempt a smile came on Noah's face, and suddenly the language came. It poured out for about five minutes, sending the animals into stitches of laughter. The teacher then asked the boy to try the script again. The result was remarkable. He was now nearly Noah.

Remarks about the Age-range Thirteen to Fifteen Years

Boys and Girls

From thirteen to fifteen years it appears to be less harmful for young actors to play before an audience. Before that it is likely to destroy absorption and sincerity, particularly if adults are present. They always laugh at the wrong moments.

Also, from thirteen to fifteen years, place great store by created documentary plays arising out of discussions around personal and social problems. It is a more intellectual way of *playing-out* and preparing for life situations.

It is not always easy to get boys to mix with the girls. But it is worth taking some things separately and mixing them on other occasions. In any case success will come by taking care to discuss or allot tasks appropriate for boys or girls.

Example—From a Visit to a Mixed School

In this group they are now used to moving together. They have done some dance work and some productions of plays. Now they are making up their own drama.

This story is about a war. There are two atomic armies, one from Earth, the other from Mars. The boys become soldiers, and the girls make hospitals in one corner of the hall and munitions factories in another. (Although in an age of emancipation and equality of the sexes one hardly

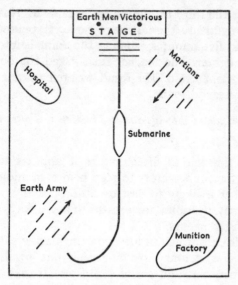

Diagram E

dares to say so, the girls have taken appropriate tasks—or what they think are so—and the boys have taken a natural lead in the stronger parts.)

There is a lot of fighting to the *Planets* (Holst), but finally a submarine cruises down the length of the hall, sprayed with "anti-Mars" so the ray-guns cannot hurt it. Despite the weeping women in one corner, weeping for the dead, Mars is captured and Earthmen stand victorious on the stage. (See Diagram E.)

The complication at this age is that girls mature more swiftly and often desire the companionship of older men. Everything should be done to aid lads in the school to face this situation and, without unduly hurrying their development, pointing out the need for cleanliness and good manners will often help them to grow up and be more acceptable to the young women. In drama, sessions of virile athletic dance and manly situations can be taken separately. When reintroduced into feminine society, the sense of achievement and personal discipline often find more favour than did the loutish teasing and laughter beforehand. Girls do not take kindly to rather ragged, rough-mannered clowns who spoil the drama period. It is up to us to help lads to understand that interest in the arts and in cleanliness need not be effeminate. There is a virile type of man to aim at. And man's art and dance should be virile. They should not be allowed to go on making the same sort of movements as women, which are often copied where boys mix with girls. It is possible for boys' drama to contain much skill and agile leaping. Leaping on and off the stage; running; leaping from rostrum block to rostrum block (and being absolutely on the time beat of music) is no mean feat. It takes skill, training, health and determination. So does musical chairs—chairs danced with at arms' length, again dead on time to music. There are many new forms of beauty and achievement for young men to find, if we help them. The man who is afraid of beauty is an oaf. (See photograph opposite page 61.)

When casting plays, an extra point to think of is not only whether the part is suitable or can be played, but is it a part they should play in order to play-out? The part is still connected with a search for the true self. It is in this way that they decide who they really are, by rejection of the characters they have played through ("I am not that person"). It will be seen that here we have to choose intelligently as to whether to consider further development of the individual or to stress the needs of theatre and the experience that can be gained from it. Both have their place.

Girls

With girls of thirteen to fifteen years, encourage dance drama with or without words. Themes for dance drama may come from the literature of the world, Greek mythology, Bible stories, etc., as a direct development from the best work by top juniors, but more detail and subtlety are included ; also the playing of music and more detailed consideration of "What does this sound remind you of?" And perhaps occasionally teachers should say what the piece reminds *them* of, but not all the time—it is the young ideas we are after, leavened only by the wisdom of age.

Anyone who has seen the exquisite spiritual quality of such imaginative work will find it less difficult to believe that this is a continuous unfolding development of an art form. (See photographs opposite pages 6o and 76.)

Example—From Work taken with Girls Fourteen to Fifteen Years

This group had been playing romantic stories about princes, journeys and success, so they were tried out with something I had used with disturbed children. It was interesting to see how these normal ones used the same age-old theme as did the others.

Self: "Just think for a moment what it might be like to be very ugly—like the ugly sisters—and you look in a big mirror. What would you feel?"

Answers: "Sad." "Fed up."

Self: "Yes, you might feel either of those. But now, as you watch, you see yourself slowly becoming beautiful and you step through the mirror into a magic new land where all your best wishes come true."

We developed this idea through discussion, and had some tense and most wonderful moments, as fairy music

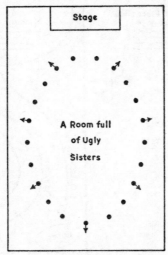

Diagram F

faded in and the girls changed from purposely ugly to a sort of radiant spiritual beauty. They stepped daintily through the imaginary mirrors and immediately began to dance all over the room in an enchanted way. Then we started on their wishes. They became rich, they married handsome artists and starved, they were rushed off (or rather danced off) on swift horses, they travelled to India, Switzerland, London and New York. They waltzed, they skated, they flew.

Never in one short period have I been transported into the realms of so gracious a kingdom of Pandora-box dreams. For one swift time, all too short, youth and hope were one with reality. Then the enchantment dimmed a little; the clock was intruding, and like a thin piece of cold steel I "faded in"[1] the fairy music of the spell. The golden

[1] i.e. Carefully brought in appropriate music on gramophone by increasing sound on the volume control.

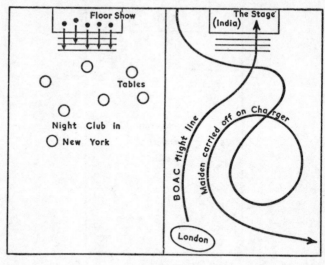

Diagram F1   Diagram F2

light died from their faces, they stepped with courage but loathing back into reality, and we were left with a room full of ugly old maids with expressions like cross-eyed codfish, till the ugly sisters changed again to become normal and gay young women. (See Diagrams F, F1 and F2.)

Boys (see photographs opposite pages 37 and 52)

Do everything possible to avoid their curious pride in being clumsy and lacking in all culture, which they mistake for manliness. Develop semi-stylised dance through imaginative situations, and work off fighting instincts by use of imagined weapons. There may be an amusing forfeit for anyone who actually lays a hand on someone else. The imagined weapon keeps an extra foot of distance between each boy and the next. Discussions lead to literature and considerations of history.

Example

Self: "Are you cold?"

Boys: "Yes."

Self: "Well, John, you take this cymbal. The rest of you, pair off. Now you are knights in armour. You have a battle axe or a big sword. [See that it is understood that it is an imagined weapon.] And you are fighting the other bloke. You have got to win. What would you do?"

A boy: "Clout 'im."

Self: "Yes! But only with the imagined axe, mind. No actual touching. Are you ready? I want to see plenty of energy. Go!"

Fighting starts. It will be ragged, perhaps, and there will be some laughter.

Self: "Right. Not bad. This time a bit more serious. Think what you are doing. Think very hard who you are, and know where you will aim. Remember, you've *got to win*. And, John, you make the clashing noises. Go!"

N.B.—This is exactly what we did in the infant school, but at a slightly different intellectual level. The deep, simple things in Child Drama should be experienced at one time. Better late than never. They fight. It is better.

Self: "Good. That's very life-like. Warmer yet?"

Boys: "Yes."

Self: "Now, this time I want you to try to do it in a steady time-beat. Listen to John making the clash. Try it first, John. You hear it? Right, ready? Go."

They fight in a semi-stylised way. Each blow is more thoughtful and already means more as art than the first laughing buffoonery. Steps could be added to this and a simple dance evolved. I would add record music, too, of an exciting nature or for a march of warriors. But today I am not doing that.

Self: "Good. I notice most of you are hacking away without placing your blows. What do you think are the weak places in the armour?"

Discussion is stimulated. I would then show them pictures which I had brought with me of knights in armour or life in Norman times, and we might lead on to literature. I would read them short pieces about the period by authors I want them to know, and they would read, too. We should not spend time here on improving the reading, but would push on to the emotional content, and improvise scenes so as to live, "do" and "struggle" what we had read about. I should take care to bring in various points of chivalry and fair play, and link them with modern examples as in, say, sport, and general opportunities for good manners.

Various people would have the opportunity of making "the sounds" if they wished. For a few minutes at the end I would let them build up a good dramatic finish on any improvised scene they wished. *Reason:* Most of the lesson had been developed intentionally on *my* lines, and I want to give reasonable opportunity for robust, self-chosen acting on *their* lines so as to ensure that the period ends happily for all of them.

For both Boys and Girls: Social Drama

With both sexes include discussions and improvisations on scenes from life to aid them in behaviour and in being explicit.

Examples

Welcoming a stranger to the school.
Entering the head's room.
Asking the boss for a rise.
Being chairman of a meeting.
Helping blind people across a road.
Being courageous in an unpleasant moral situation.
Telling people the way.
Asking a girl for a dance.
Being asked for a dance.
Emergency calls for aid to firemen or police.

Also we would discuss clothes of past periods and arrive at taste in present times, considering cleanliness and choice of colour—all of immense secret importance to the adolescent, giving rise sometimes to violent behaviour if not sympathetically dealt with.

Example (see photographs opposite page 77)

In a crowded classroom the master was taking some social drama—that is, drama concerned obviously with everyday life and how it affects us. He was helping them to think about what life would be like when they had left school.

Master: "I want you to imagine that you are going for your first job and you are being interviewed by the boss of a firm. It is very important for you to appear at your best."

Some boys were sorted out and told to talk things over for a few minutes. They then used the master's end of the room as the office and he lent his desk for the boss to sit at. There followed the most incredible version of what an interview of this kind is like. The candidate for the job was brought in by, seemingly, two prison warders, and flung into the room. The boss slept with his feet on the table, and his foreman conducted the interview like a scene from the Inquisition. Ten applicants were tortured and no one got the job. Some of the remarks were:

"'Ow much pay jer want?"

"Thousand dollars a week."

"Kaw, you can't be any good; we only pay two thousand 'ere."

Again—

"'Ow much jer want?"

"Fifteen pound."

"A month?"

"No, a week."

"Wot, a little tich like you? Take 'im away and screw 'is arm off."

After a few such trials the master began to look at me with a strange countenance. His expression was a mixture of apology and despair, with a dash of apprehension in it—apprehension at what I might be thinking. All right, I thought. Education is largely a matter of compassion. So I began to take over.

Self: "Right. Now, let's talk about this. Remember, you are going for your first job. Would you want to be thrown into the room or not?"

A few answers of "No". They were weighing me up.

Self: "Do you think you really would be?"

Answers: "Dunno, sir." "No, sir." "Not if you was to be'ave, sir."

Self: "No, I think you can take it pretty well for certain that that won't happen to you. Now, what would happen?"

By now they were giving full attention, so I

started to make the situation as personal as possible for each boy.

Self: "It is really you, each one of you, going for your first job. How do you think you should look and behave?"

Answers came pouring forth: "Look clean!" "Tidy 'air, sir!" "Stand well!" "Be polite like!" "Answer well!"

Self: "Yes, that's grand. That's more like it, isn't it? Now, the boss? Do you think he would really sleep like that? If the employee was going to take his money, wouldn't he try and see the person asking for the job and judge him carefully? I think, too, that he might want to ask some of the questions himself. In a very big firm the boss might not be there at all himself except when taking people into very high positions. His representative might do the job. But, anyway, I doubt if he would have a sort of foreman-executioner to do it.

"Now, let's try it again. Last time you were making a sort of cartoon of the situation, like something out of a comic. That's all right. It was fun and very believable in places. [Notice how to keep their sympathy by not destroying faith in their first attempt. Always lead; don't crush.] But let's make it more real now, more true to what is really going to happen to you in a year or so's time. This is quite serious grown-up stuff now."

They did the same again, and there were several changes of cast. In one case I suggested a reversal of roles to let the boss feel how long he had left standing a man seeking a senior post. We finally became deeply immersed in discussion about manners, cleanliness, thought for others, the boss's position and his care for the workers, and on their side what they owed the boss, or the firm, in hard work, loyalty and cooperation in return for a fair wage. No one had given

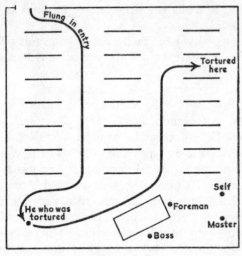

Diagram G

these lads a firm picture of what the getting of a job really means or entails. It was a session of drama which somehow led us all nearer to manhood, and a finer maturity too. (See Diagram G.)

It may be found that some form of social drama in this sense is the best way to start things off with older children who have already become self-conscious. They have a spurious contempt for art as such, but if neither the words *drama* nor *theatre* were stressed they might be very prepared to discuss and practise preparation for life, and particularly life after school. It makes them feel grown-up. Once having become released, they can be more easily introduced to other parts of drama as a whole.

GENERAL REMARKS—*All Ages Five to Fifteen Years*

The general qualities, throughout the whole age range, which can be considered *dramatic* criteria:

Sincerity, absorption, surety, robust outflow of verbal expression, sensitivity, recognition and variation of mood, attunement to situation, conscious joy in movement and rhythm, believability.

Try to develop all of these.

Speech criteria: Clarity, sincerity, good flow of language, joy in the sound, contrast and mood.

It is joy in all sound which can be obtained by the constant use of noises. This brings out the emotional love at the root of all language, and is a surer way of securing taste than saying "that author is good". If the ear is trained, the child hears what is good, and there is less artificial glorification of an author's name. Long sounds and short ones begin appreciation of the function of vowel and consonant. Only worry about accent in very special cases; this belongs to formal training and is done separately. In Child Drama one tries to develop the genuine self as found. Interference breaks confident flow. Regularity is more important in effect than indiscriminately arranged long periods; even the twenty minutes' lesson can be of value if taken each week.

Children's Theatre

One obvious repercussion of an acceptance of Child Drama is its considerable effect on children's theatre. It becomes necessary to provide certain forms of theatre that are in sympathy with Child Drama, and there are now a few adult groups in England that seriously endeavour to do so. In general terms it is a question of adults, if they play to children, presenting plays in the shapes (relevant to age) that appear in Child Drama, encouraging audience participation and including interesting noises.

Films[1] have a different influence altogether and do not affect shape-consciousness in the same way as theatre does.

What do we learn from all this?

Let's first consider what the child thinks:

The Child as Teacher

In approaching Child Drama, the best results are obtained by believing that the child is not only an original artist but an important person. With this in mind, I hold discussions with children. In and out of school, always discuss, particularly out-of-school, when frank answers are obtained. One learns much from this.

The following are questions that I have put to children under eleven years of age:

Question: "When did you start to act?"

Answer: "When I was a baby."

Question: "What's the best age to start the sort of acting we do together?"

Answer: "Young 'as is everest possible."

Question: "Do your teachers teach you to act?"

Answer: "Yes, some of them talk at you all the time. You don't. It's better then, 'cos you really know what to do before you start."

Another child: "Talking stops you doing things."

Question: "Do you like your own plays or ones that have been written by other people?"

Answer: "Ours is best."

Question: "If you got stuck when you were playing would

[1] Films and children's theatre are discussed fully in *Child Drama*, Part III, Chapters XVI and XIX.

Beginning of adult theatre: This is a floor show in an imaginary night club at Rea Street Drama Centre. Note mime of band on the stage

Secondary Modern girls: Dance drama (see p. 66)

Social drama: Top class Senior boys practising, through drama, how to behave at interviews. The "boss" is very absorbed in the imaginary credentials of the candidate

Social drama: Serious discussion with the teacher on the interviews shown in the photograph above (see pp. 70–74)

you like to be left alone, or is it nice if a grown-up helps you?"

Answer: "It's nice to finish, but it must be a *nice* grown-up or it's not nice. Some grown-ups aren't nice about helping. They tell you what to do too much."

Question: "Do you like lots of ideas for stories to act, or a few?"

Answer: "Just a few."

Question: "And long ideas or short?"

Answer: "Just little ideas. You can make them big after."

Question: "Do you like to have acting just sometimes at school, or often?"

Answer: "It would be nice if acting was in all subjects."

Question: "What would you prefer the teacher to do when you are acting your own plays?"

Answer: "Just watch—except if you like the teacher *very* much they could join in just sometimes."

Question: "If you were acting a play about history and someone stopped you to tell you how the people you were acting behaved a long time ago, would you like it?"

Answer: "No, I'd think they were interruptin'—and I wouldn't listen, either."

Question: "Oh! Would you pretend to listen?"

Answer: "Yes."

Question: "Why?"

Answer: "Because I wouldn't want them to know."

Question: "Why?"

Answer: "Afraid I'd get into trouble."

(Formal producers take heed.)

Question: "Some teachers want to help you very much. Do you like it when they do?"

Answer: "Depends what they do. I don't like how they do it at my school."

Question: "How do they do it?"

Answer: "Tell you how you ought to act it like."

Question: "Isn't that nice?"

Answers: 1. "No. I think they're stopping me."

2. "It doesn't help."

Question: "Do you like music on when you are acting?"

Answer: "Yes, it tells you when to be puppies or fairies or when the enemy is coming."

Question: "If you couldn't think of something, would you like someone to suggest a story, or would it be annoying?"

Answers: 1. "Yes, I'd like it."

2. "It's nice to be helped when you *can't* use a gun or a sword, but while you're trying it's as annoying as a—a kick."

Question: "Does acting help you to know things?"

Answer (seven-year-old): "Yes, I'm sure I know a lot about life, 'cos I act so much. I'm alwiz *being* someone."

Question: "Do you get acting at school like we do it here?"

Answer: "No, it's a pity, most of our teachers don't let us act. They keep suggesting all the time."

Question: "Do you find it nice to act this way?"

Answer: "Yes."

Question: "Is it easy?"

Answers: 1. "Yes. You sort of mean it more."

2. "It's easy to act when you're here. *You* don't stop and ask why we did it like that or tell us things all the time."

3. "I can't *never* do it like this wiv our teacher. She says it's silly."

In summing-up, one might say that early Child Drama is such as to be an absorbed playing-outwards from self all round and in all directions, and needs no audience.

Later, as the child approaches proscenium theatre, personality projection takes place as usual, but this should happen slowly.

Genuine Child Drama has an ascetic quality, and is more often at its best without property, dress or setting. The enemy of Child Drama is credit for the teacher, which tends to warp everything for personal glory or that of the school. I am well aware that acceptance of these ideas would, in some places, make for something of a revolution in drama as education, but that they are gaining favour is undoubted by the testimony of many who work with children. The Educational Drama Association uses these methods and develops the ideas better than I could alone. By its aid, and as a result of the first book,[1] people have been making enquiries from all over the world, sending me descriptions of their experiments in these methods at schools, clinics, prisons, or in just ordinary homes.

This is an opinion, similar to many, expressed by one head teacher:

"I thought it was just talk at first, but I don't now. I should never have believed Child Drama would make such a difference to the children and to the atmosphere of my school. This at last is liberty without licence."

And here is the opinion of a backward boy who was asked about Child Drama: "God, man, 'tis the *only thing*."

Some people like facts and figures. Others get annoyed with them. If you put them in you are thought to be trying to prove too much. If you leave them out you are being impractical. For those who like them it might be of interest that in one particular year I estimated (fairly conservatively) that I had had some personal contact with over thirty-two thousand children under fourteen. (A critic of my other book took it that I had written a

[1] *Child Drama.*

questionnaire to this number of children. I mean, of course, that I had met them, talked with them, seen them play, or actually played with them.)

Of these thirty-two thousand, three said they preferred the script play to their own Child Drama.

After Childhood

This book is only an introduction, but enough may have been said for it to be seen that the attitude which makes Child Drama possible need not, indeed does not always, die. But many young people in youth clubs show unmistakable signs in their characters of the lack of this training. However, it is quite possible to hold with them sessions of imaginative drama which are akin to the work described and which replaces something of the years that have been lost. Even adults can be helped to create seriously, too. Older people naturally do their best at a different intellectual level, that is all.

It has been my great privilege to have created imaginative spontaneous drama with almost every type and age of person, from healthy as well as maladjusted children to delinquent boys, from teachers and architects to professional actors, from male Army groups to Women's Land Army, from Day Continuation school students and adult factory groups to directors of industry, and from Women's Institutes to old men's clubs. Descriptions of these further stages of work and the exciting theatre that arises out of them are now being prepared for publication also. In the meantime, suffice it to say that Child Drama aids young individuals to discover peace and confidence for themselves and share it with others, to become open and loyal and to do a good job of work. Grown-ups find peace, too, and discover new realms of expression. It is necessary to aid them to confidence, for so many of us are ashamed of beauty. We seem to think it should be put away with other childish things. But it is an adult thing, too, only with adults it is more conscious. It belongs to the deepest forms of civilisation and imparts sincerity to our being. At least let us see that succeeding generations do not suffer from our own self-consciousness. We miss so much. Let us help them to find the natural treasure that is theirs by right.

CHAPTER VI

QUESTIONS AND ANSWERS

1. *Is improvisation more important than theatre training?*

It *is* theatre training as well as education, and is the basis of Child Drama. Doing plays is not always good theatre training or education.

2. *Is there more projected play than personal play in the earlier years?*

Yes, a great deal from one to four years, as the child is not yet a good mover. Personal play, i.e. being the character oneself, develops more as walking and running are achieved with confidence. Obviously it is no fun "being" someone if you're going to fall down all the time. You need most of your mind to help you to stay upright in the first years of life.

3. *Should the young child have many properties to play with?*

Do not overload it when finding its way towards acting and other things through personal play. Genuine Child Drama relies on inner creation, not outer materialism.

4. *Should we encourage children to talk while miming?*

Yes, whenever they wish, though with the younger child much speech comes through the body. Gesture is language; so is pulling faces. Occasions of "do it without talking this time" are of value for concentration on movement. But speech cannot start too early. Too much music and movement inhibits speech.

5. *Should teacher or child choose the cast?*

Both should have a say, sometimes one more than the other; tiny children are, of course, less able to do so. Children are at times capable of choosing and grow to be good critics of each other's work, but in more polished improvisations the teacher may have to organise a little. Teachers learn to *feel* what is needed.

6. *Is the twenty-minute lesson possible?*

Even only twenty minutes a week helps. Play in short bursts is valuable and is often obtainable where children have trust and are unafraid. Learning to be quick is part of the training this work brings.

7. *Should a teacher show a child how to move?*

If the teacher does, it is not Child Drama. If imagination fails, give some suggestion on *what* to do but not *how* to do it.

8. *Would you make a suggestion while play is going on?*

Interruptions tend to shake confidence. If an adult interferes too often, Child Drama dies. This is different from sensitive, well-timed suggestion.

9. *Does this training militate against the usual education and child training?*

It need not. Some periods of creative play have been of value even in the most formal schools. Periods of games and P.E. are considered a useful balance. Drama, sensibly used, has the same effect. It makes children more friendly, open and direct, and the habit of absorption achieved in this training is the best way of learning concentration for all forms of study.

10. *Should teachers have experience in improvisation themselves?*

Yes, I run courses for this purpose. We meet, move, speak together, and every teacher takes the group.[1]

11. *Is the ordinary teacher qualified to take Child Drama?*

Ordinary teachers who are human beings are the *best* people to do this work. If they learn about drama, they may be better at it, but not necessarily. However, if you are taking maladjusted or delinquent children you need to be more experienced.

12. *What would you expect to find in good Child Drama lessons?*

They should be joyful, in an encouraging atmosphere. The teacher should be keen, quiet, kindly, observant, and know how to stimulate if necessary. There should be variety and new creation, clear defined shapes in movement and good use of space. Questions should be answered adequately, suggestions encouraged and used. There should be complete control, with good contrast—noise and quiet. Speech should be flowing, rapid and unhesitating, of poetic and philosophic language between six and ten, and increasingly witty and gay between ten and fifteen. There should be zest in the acting, good group sensitivity, marked sincerity and absorption, bringing high moments of "theatre". I would hope to see things, animals, people or movements I had not thought of, and an example of "running play". The unconscious grouping would be exciting. Everybody would get an equal chance of creation.

That would be a pretty good lesson. The teacher would

[1] It is essential that colleges of education should now include Child Drama courses or that there should be a main separate course.

not teach, but guide and nurture; he, too, has to be a creative artist, constantly ready to offer aid if needed.

There are no short cuts to this work, no hard or easy rules. Each child is different, and each teacher learns to handle things his own way. Before starting we must love the child, love the work, and know why we do it. If we cannot at all times love, because of tiredness, then we must develop a deep sense of justice. For at the root of all creative opportunity lies an elementary justice for the child. Together with the child a wisdom is built, and an emotional sharing experienced. Out of this grows the indefinable knowledge of life that constitutes for the child *education* in the full sense of the word.

13. *How can all the class participate in the limited space of a classroom?*

Allow the main players to approach those sitting in desks; buying and selling can go on in this way, or a fugitive can ask for cover under a desk. Everyone can join in with effects noises, tapping of pencils for rain or leaves on the window, desk lids for explosions, chubby fists for feet of unknown animals, and whistling and sighing for wind.

14. *Is there noise when first starting this work?*

Sometimes. Older boys make noise, particularly if they have not had much freedom. But they soon learn that undue noise spoils creation. Thus the personal responsibility for restraint is slowly *passed over* to them.

15. *If not too confident about keeping control in the hall, what should a teacher do?*

It is sometimes better to use less space first. By grouping the class in a ring and letting relays of players work in the centre you keep conditions similar to the classroom.

The ring can be enlarged as desired, and more players take part, until the whole group is able to take part all over the room. Quiet and control are thus built slowly, though noise is often necessary to good drama at certain climaxes.

16. *Children who leave the junior school often grow self-conscious. What can we do?*

The self-consciousness is connected with puberty, and one of its causes is the break in atmosphere and teaching approach in the senior school, where continuity of method is needed for at least the first year. We must give *more* opportunity. It is largely our fault if self-consciousness prevails.

17. *How do you cope with the able and dominating child?*

Without cramping its leadership, ensure that others get a chance by sometimes suggesting that other children do leading jobs. If the leadership is constructive, leave it.

18. *Why are children shy in school but not in their play outside?*

Sometimes because of previous experience of adults—this may not be the teacher's fault but that of the parent. It is sometimes due to the atmosphere of the school. In some schools fear is still the main force. Where fear of restraint is the only understood form of discipline, you get rowdy play outside and anything from shyness to despair inside.

19. *Would you "make" a shy child join in?*

Never. If present at regular play sessions, he will join in at the *only moment when it is absolutely right and proper for him to do so*—that is at the moment he *wants* to. A long and courageous battle precedes this, but there should be encouragement. The teacher's common sense decides on the need, just as when setting sums.

20. *How does this work go with "C" children?*

Very well. They find hope and happiness in Child Drama. Sometimes it is their only opportunity for success, and so is very important for them.

21. *What would you do if a difficult child started to break up the group?*

It is hard to generalise—each child is different. But here are some suggestions: First try giving responsibility. Make the child the arch-good or arch-evil character. If overdone, quell by giving a more important part to someone else. Remember there is a reason for the behaviour, often a symptom of a longing for expression—so opportunity is what is needed. If in doubt, keep near the child; physical nearness often helps. If behaviour improves, slowly move farther away, so that responsibility for self-discipline is almost imperceptibly taken over by the child. If behaviour still does not improve (very unlikely), remove the opportunity of expressing and of being leader, and invent a static character like a lamp or tree, first left alone, then, if necessary, getting the play moving round the child so that it feels itself to be the centre again. By alternating obvious, less obvious, and no responsibility, you are likely to get a changed reaction. Speak strongly only as the second resort, and deal strongly as the last resort.

22. *Why is acting on a stage bad for young children?*

Because it destroys Child Drama, and children then merely try to copy what adults call theatre. They are not successful in this, and it is not their way of playing. They need space, and don't need to be embroiled in the complicated technique of an artificial theatre form. It makes them conscious of audience, spoils their sincerity and teaches them to show off.

23. *Isn't an audience necessary for some plays?*

For set plays it may be. For Child Drama it isn't. We mustn't muddle them up.

24. *What about hearing the speech?*

At first adult judgment would often say speech is poor, because: (*a*) practice and confidence in speaking at all is badly needed; (*b*) words are invented that do not appear in our dictionary; (*c*) a local accent may be used. Speech becomes louder and clearer in time. A hint dropped once in two or three weeks about being a little louder is often enough to have a marked effect.

25. *What about choral speech?*

It can help children to discover team spirit and group sensitivity, if they are not discovering these things in other ways. Experts sometimes obtain good results, but it is a complicated form of art and non-experts induce into the children's voices a dead whine, which often remains in all their public speaking. It is the same unnatural sound that comes from attempting script plays too early. Forms of group outcry and unconscious agreement of group sentences occur occasionally during Child Drama, and later can be a basis for choral speech, which should not be imposed on children too early. When great choirs of children chant earnest poems at adults in public, one is often at a loss to know what the point is, either as education or training in taste. Perhaps it is best used for class groups. The only way of keeping speech sincere and full of life is by lots of improvisation going side by side with it. Voice is an individual thing and should not be confined only to herd utterance. I am not condemning choral speech as such—only challenging its unthoughtful use by inexpert trainers. Sometimes it is the only speech-training children get, and that is harmful.

26. *Would you advocate moving to jingles?*

No. Be careful not to overstress rhyme; it often causes children to think poetry is sloppy trash later in life. Children have a deep sense of poetry in their own minds, but their own poetry does not rhyme. Rhyme is something which is brought to their attention by adults, and then copied. They may learn to think they love rhyme, and will, in early stages, tell you rhymes by the dozen; these rhymes, by the way, usually do not rhyme. But once they have really got the rhyme craze and know how to do it, they lose confidence in creating in their own way. Their poetry, at its best, is more akin to the Bible and the "moderns", psalm-like in character, or like T. S. Eliot in shape, kaleidoscopic like Laurie Lee, or soulfully moving like the translations by Spender of Garcia Lorca. Thus they find plenty of opportunity of expressing many ideas, which may be full of conscious joy or unconscious dream symbolism. Once the disease of rhyme has been badly caught, all poetic expression shrivels into the meagre canal of the rhyming ballad, and may remain thus for many years, perhaps for ever. There is a "Child Poetry", and it is for teachers and parents to recognise this, without emotional outcry, and to develop it as they learn how.

27. *When should children do script plays?*

For the average child, at about thirteen years of age. In any case not until they can *read really well*, with *meaning* and understand what they are saying. Before this, scripts are harmful as they teach the child the appalling habit of never getting into the part and of reciting lines whilst grinning at the audience. There is no educational, theatre, nor dramatic value in this. Do not think that they are learning to appreciate good English this way. They are not thinking of what they do or say.

28. *When children have had only formal proscenium drama, how would you start?*

Continue with plays as they know them. Begin to use other entrances in the hall. Let the children flow on and off the stage. Use processions round the hall. When part of the play is unsatisfactory, let them play it in dumb show, or begin to say in their own words what they would say if the event happened in their own lives. Build, in fact, slowly back to what they should have been doing, and bring in as many children as possible. With older children, who are ready for plays, anyway, some improvisation should also be done regularly. It adds a sparkle to their work and keeps them mentally alert.

29. *How do you link improvisation with the play later?*

True improvisation comes first, then a polished improvisation, which is getting nearer to a play. Then sometimes words or sentences are written down to help keep an outline of the play. Later, the whole or nearly all a play is written down. Stories are written parallel with this, and finally we launch on to their own attempts at a script play, and study of plays by adults.

30. *What about young children writing plays?*

Never discourage, but young children often write better if encouraged merely to write stories about their experiences during improvisation. Their written plays are generally rather bad and as disappointing to them as to us when acted. Their improvised plays are better. Over thirteen or so, their script plays evolve well.

31. *Is Shakespeare possible in the secondary modern school?*

Yes, but as far as Child Drama is concerned it would come into the category of the script play. Many much older actors are incapable of either understanding or acting Shakespeare, though I have seen fourteen- and fifteen-year-olds get at some of the poetic essence of Shakespeare. Use improvisation on the plot of the play first. When zest for the story and characters is aroused, try the script. Don't be afraid to select and edit.

32. *Does Child Drama help in discovering the correct approach to every school subject?*

Certainly it will when fully understood. I have not yet discovered any subject which cannot be approached by some form of dramatic method. But chiefly it is valuable as preparing the personality for co-operation in study.

33. *How does this work apply to grammar schools?*

It is difficult for grammar schools to fit it in because they are pressed for time, and many teachers feel that the intelligent child does not need it. This is a mistake, as even the clever person is a child, too, in part, and will undoubtedly miss something without this training. They may become clever, but quite unsound on moral judgments later in life. There are also those who have been either wrongly streamed or lack confidence by having fallen behind in their studies. Child Drama is essential for them. Universities are beginning to ask what should be done with young people who have specialised to such an extent that the other part of their mind is undeveloped. It is beginning to be felt that much important training is being left out somewhere. The drama that I nave advocated for children between twelve and eighteen years might apply to grammar schools, particularly in the sphere of social drama. And even if one is only considering the standard of production in their formal presentation of theatre, why should the clever child miss the proper training that his brother and sister are receiving more generally now in other schools? Even young professsionals are beginning to receive it, too.

34. *Wouldn't the same apply then to preparatory schools, public schools and private schools in general?*

Yes, some representative associations of these schools are already asking for courses; and in some of these schools very imaginative and exciting drama now takes place. They have begun to find that children are still children and thrive on natural creative opportunity. They still pass their exams.

35. *When did you first think of drama as therapy?*

About 1926. I developed this further whilst abroad, with the help of expert advice, and began serious experiments in 1931, developing it further, with medical advice, from 1938 to 1941. During this time I felt what I personally had been convinced of for a number of years to have been proved, namely that prevention is better than cure and the introduction of simple play methods into the normal school curriculum would bring about a natural, happy development with a considerable balancing effect on character, the building of confidence, and an improvement in scholastic attainment and taste generally. But since 1953 I have given more time to delinquency and maladjustment again.

36. *Can you give suggestions on the curative value of drama?*

Children who suffer from nightmares can be helped to face their fears through play, and the dreams may disappear afterwards. Children and adults suffering from pain will, when acting out a story, often perform movements which they cannot do in cold blood. Thinking of something else helps them. Realisation of their achievement brings hope and confidence, and the actual inducing of the movement may be necessary to the cure. Building of confidence by acting little scenes, like having to go into a shop and buy things, is useful, too, after certain forms of treatment. The patient slowly finds the courage to face the world again. Children who are backward or upset obtain release through creative drama, and often mix with their fellows again afterwards, in realising that they got on perfectly well in dance or play. Legitimate opportunity to act out a character that haunts or tempts, particularly during adolescence, can save a young person from actually becoming the character in real life. They face and choose, this way, their course of conduct. Dramatic play is used as an aid to diagnosis in child guidance clinics and also, in part, for curative purposes. I think the wider use of drama will prove of great value as prevention quite apart from therapy.

37. *Do you advocate masks for younger children?*

Yes, occasionally. Part-masks are better, as they allow eye and mouth freedom and yet still provide a fascinating experience. Full masks help shy children, but are rather hot. Masks with no noses are cooler, and there is a special joy for each child in choosing what colour to dab on its own nose.

38. *Do you believe in make-up for the child?* [1]

At times. Let them develop their own art form in this and do not instruct until they begin to ask questions—at about twelve years or later. Child art in make-up is sometimes connected with the action which precedes or follows in the form of Child Drama. One may stimulate the other. Another part of child make-up is like painting a picture—acting does not then come into it at all. But vivid spots, stripes and patterns may be put on the face. Allow this.

39. *Can children make their own music?*

Yes, and it might be developed much further. When children have been unusually delighted by a drama or dance experience they make sounds to accompany themselves. It is a spontaneous outburst, either singly or of a group. They make delightful musical instruments of their own too. No doubt books will soon be written on Child Music.

40. *Is there any association one can join which helps teachers, parents and actors to know more about Child Drama and imaginative theatre generally, and advises on developing this work?*

Anyone requiring further information should write to me direct, c/o The Education Office, Birmingham [England], or through the International Theatre Institute.

[1] Masks and make-up are discussed fully in *Child Drama*.

INDEX

(A photograph is referred to by means of bold type, indicating the page opposite to which the illustrations will be found)